IN DEFENCE
OF CANADA

IN DEFENCE OF CANADA

Reflections of a Patriot

MICHEL MAISONNEUVE

TORONTO, 2024

Sutherland House
416 Moore Ave., Suite 304
Toronto, ON M4G 1C9

Copyright © 2024 by Michel Maisonneuve

All rights reserved, including the right to reproduce this book or portions thereof in any form whatsoever. For information on rights and permissions or to request a special discount for bulk purchases, please contact Sutherland House at sutherlandhousebooks@gmail.com

Sutherland House and logo are registered trademarks of The Sutherland House Inc.

First edition, November 2024

If you are interested in inviting one of our authors to a live event or media appearance, please contact sranasinghe@sutherlandhousebooks.com and visit our website at sutherlandhousebooks.com for more information.

We acknowledge the support of the Government of Canada.

Manufactured in Canada
Cover designed by Leah Ciani, Shalomi Ranasinghe, and Jordan Lunn
Book composed by Karl Hunt

Library and Archives Canada Cataloguing in Publication
Title: In defence of Canada / Michel Maisonneuve.
Names: Maisonneuve, Michel, author.
Identifiers: Canadiana (print) 20240415019 | Canadiana (ebook) 20240415051 | ISBN 9781990823954 (hardcover) | ISBN 9781990823961 (EPUB)
Subjects: LCSH: National characteristics, Canadian. | LCSH: Exceptionalism—Canada. | LCSH: Social change—Canada. | LCSH: Political participation—Canada.
Classification: LCC FC95.5 .M347 2024 | DDC 306.0971—dc23

ISBN 978-1-990823-95-4
eBook 978-1-990823-96-1

Contents

Acknowledgements		vii
	Introduction	1
1	Becoming	10
2	Canada's Glorious Past	17
3	Canada Exits the World's Stage	27
4	Radical Agendas	46
5	DEI, Democracy, and Meritocracy	59
6	The Climate and Our Resources	70
7	The Economy in Crisis	80
8	Immigration	86
9	The Military	97
10	Veterans	132
11	How to Move Forward	143
	Conclusion	165
	About the Author	167

Acknowledgements

THIS BOOK WOULD HAVE never come together without the support and help of my wife, Major (ret'd) Barbara Krasij. Throughout our time together, she has been my protector, my best friend, my foil, my common-sense expert, my best editor, and the love of my life: thank you.

Thanks also to Andrea Douglas and Dave Roberts for their constant support and sound advice, as well as my family for their love and support.

After my speech on receiving the Vimy Award in November 2022, the *National Post* was the only news outlet that dared publish my speech and subsequently gave me a forum for comments. I am grateful to Postmedia, and especially to Carson Jerema and his team. Thank you to my agent Brian J. Wood for introducing me to the literary world, and to Ken Whyte and the entire team at Sutherland House for taking a chance on me and making my work better.

Finally, thank you to all those who wrote or called to support me after my speech and every time I wrote an opinion piece. You gave me hope after I was cancelled.

*To the silent majority of Canadians, old or new,
who want to work to make our country better.
Let's be silent no longer.*

Introduction

IT IS SEPTEMBER 2023. I am behind a curtain with my wife Barbara, waiting to take the stage to deliver the keynote speech at the opening of the Conservative Party of Canada's convention in Quebec City. I can hear the emcees reading parts of our biographies. There is a buzz in the crowd of 2,500 attendees, and the speech is going to be broadcast live on television. I wasn't really nervous, but I *was* asking myself, "How the hell did I get here?"

I had retired in 2018 after spending forty-six years in the military and public service. For many years, I had been thinking about the state of our country. Especially since 2015, when Justin Trudeau was elected as prime minister, I had been unhappy with the direction Canada was headed. Many things grated on me: no unifying vision, a lack of courage in our leaders, too large a focus on climate change and almost none on our natural resources, the dominance of cultural and gender issues, decimation (again) of our Canadian Armed Forces, and the constant apologies for our history.

In 2020, I was informed I had won the Vimy Award, recognizing me as a "Canadian who has made a significant and outstanding contribution to the defence and security of Canada and the preservation of (its) democratic values." This was considered to be a lifetime achievement award, recognizing not only my thirty-five years in uniform, but my

INTRODUCTION

subsequent decade in the public service and years championing veterans' causes and supporting the growth of our country.

The dinner where I was to be presented with the award was postponed several times due to the COVID-19 pandemic, and the ongoing events continued to exacerbate my feeling of disillusionment with national affairs. Most obviously, deficit spending by the government was out of control. I felt we abandoned and ultimately sacrificed those in long-term care during the pandemic. It was unacceptable that they were dying alone, terrified, confused, uncared for and in filthy diapers, while the rest of us masked up and stayed in our social bubbles. They deserved so much better than we gave them.

There was virtue signalling of all kinds, starting with our prime minister, who had abandoned the social distancing he decreed and knelt with the Black Lives Matter demonstrators in June 2020. When criticized, he defended himself, saying, "I felt it was important for me to be part of that . . . To be able to listen, to be able to hear people and to be able to understand and to share with people how important it was to act." How unfortunate he didn't feel the same need to "listen and hear people and be able to understand" when the Freedom Convoy rolled into Ottawa less than two years later. Instead, he labelled those Canadians a far-right movement, a "small fringe minority of people" with "unacceptable views." All they wanted was to be heard.

Meanwhile, the reduction of our international influence was continuing, as was the weakening of our armed forces, and the self-flagellation of our country about Indigenous residential schools, our colonial past, and our horrible history in general.

I felt our country was failing, the government was failing to lead, and I needed to take a stand. I decided that the speech at the Vimy Gala would be my platform. I saw it as a call to action and started to plan what I wanted to say. Having spent nearly five decades protecting free speech and never commenting on government policy, I felt I had earned the right to share my views on the state of our country and its future. I delivered the speech in November 2022 on a stage at the Museum of Civilization in Ottawa to an audience of some 600, including the chief justice of the Supreme Court of Canada and a mix of senior public servants and executives, military officers, academics, and businesspeople.

I knew I would be speaking in the Ottawa bubble, or more accurately, a parallel universe compared to the reality of Canadians who live outside it. Ottawa is a public service city, with jobs assured, great pension plans, and a stable future, often untouched by the economic issues facing the rest of the country. In this insular environment, I hoped to ruffle a few feathers and create a dialogue between the public service, the government, and Canadians like me who had become frustrated with the direction of policy and the destruction of the very ideals and principles I and many others had spent our lives defending.

I wanted to shock people and elicit a response. What I learned that night, and in the days and weeks that followed, is how deeply the so-called woke attitudes have penetrated all facets of our society and what it feels like to be a target of that twenty-first-century phenomenon, cancel culture. My cancellation began with a blog post by an academic who, although present at the award ceremony, declined to speak to me in person. The next day he ranted about my speech, calling me outdated and a poster boy for all that ailed the Canadian Armed Forces and its culture. The ensuing social media storm ended my professional relationship with a veterans' organization I had championed. It earned me personal rebuffs from people I knew, public denouncements, and even physical threats from people I had never met. It even ended friendships.

Interestingly, and more importantly, I was astonished by the ordinary Canadians who risked their own cancellation by stepping up to applaud my words and offer their support. The *National Post* picked up the controversy and several of their columnists supported my views and my right to voice them. The paper printed my speech and invited me to elaborate on what it called my "anti-woke" opinions. This was the first

INTRODUCTION

time a headline branded me "the anti-woke general." The response was overwhelmingly supportive. The gratitude expressed by many members of the Canadian Armed Forces, from all ranks, touched me more than I can say. Many thanked me for saying things they could not and asked me to "keep talking."

We Canadians are a complacent people. As former Canadian politician Sheila Copps said, "Canadians are generally a cautious lot . . . we are the world's neighbours and just about everybody's friends. We do not push our way to the front of the line and probably say 'sorry' and 'excuse me' more than any other nation on earth."

Maybe this complacency comes from living next door to the greatest democracy on earth, believing we are safe under its nuclear umbrella. Sometimes, though, it feels more like apathy, as if we just couldn't give a damn. We have little personal opinion about important issues. Someone once told me that, compared to the US, we never put big issues on the table and debate them. We prefer evolution, slow as it needs to be, instead of revolution. Perhaps this is because our nation was born not of revolution but evolution, with the Fathers of Confederation discussing and eventually creating the first association of provinces. The US, by contrast, was created via a bloody revolution and bound with one of the most important documents of history, The Declaration of Independence, a statement that guarantees its citizens equality, the right to life, liberty, and the pursuit of happiness, and obliges its citizens to defend those rights. It's an obligation that generations of Americans have taken seriously, thus becoming the defenders of the free world.

Not surprisingly, my name was mud with the federal Liberal government. Several of the organizations that publicly cut ties with me received all or much of their funding from that government. Even the blogger who started the cancellation was receiving federal grant money. However, within weeks of my speech, members of both the Conservative Party of Canada and the People's Party of Canada reached out to see if I would run as a federal political candidate. All this led to an eventual meeting with

Conservative leader Pierre Poilievre and a request to deliver the keynote address at the opening of the September 2023 CPC convention with my wife, Barbara, who is also an armed forces veteran.

When word got out that we would be speaking at the convention, we heard again from the same academic who had started the cancellation process. In an article published in the *Globe & Mail*, he accused the CPC of politicizing the military. I decided to write what I believe was a thoughtful rebuttal and contacted the *Globe* to see if they would print it. Surprisingly, it was declined by the *Globe* opinions editor; so much for airing both sides of an issue.

I still do not believe I was (or am) politicizing the military. I have been retired from the public service for more than five years and hung up my uniform more than seventeen years ago. I believe I am entitled to state my views, even if they do not please everyone. Many of my retired colleagues in the senior ranks of the military are happy to live out their retirement. I would be lying if I haven't wondered at times why some who could take a stand do not.

Every year of my uniformed career, the chief of defence staff (CDS) would hold a seminar in Ottawa for all serving general and flag officers. At the end of my first such seminar of my career upon being promoted to brigadier-general, the CDS asked for comments and suggestions on the annual gathering. I was a bit critical of the event, so the CDS told me "OK, then you can organize the next one" (I've used this tactic myself many times). I did, and asked those officers who had just made it to one-star rank to be prepared to describe to their peers their thoughts and feelings about joining the general ranks. All their comments reflected the fact that throughout their careers they never expected to become generals or flag officers. In addition to being a measure of their humility, this meant that we had to ensure those who had become generals would take their leadership responsibilities seriously. As a retired general, I no longer have authority, but I still feel a need to speak out and exert leadership, even if all I may have now is influence.

INTRODUCTION

Our current trajectory as a country seems to me to be downward. Canada, with its almost infinite natural resources, its tolerant and diverse population, its glorious history and endless potential, could be a true world player, capable of great things and leading in the most important areas. But to do this, we need leaders to excite national confidence and pride throughout our population. We need to stop apologizing for the past and judging history by today's standards. We need to make Canadians believe in our potential and help them realize it. And we need to harness this potential and put it to use to help Canada and the world prosper. Meekly going along with the government of the day, letting it carry on regardless of its lack of vision, and simply acquiescing to whatever underwhelming proposal is brought forth, can no longer be tolerated. We need outrage! We need ordinary Canadians involved! We need to be heard! We need to vote! And we need a government that will motivate us to be all we can be, so that Canada can truly be all it can be.

I will not go into politics. I'm too old and I don't have the energy or the staying power to put up with all the polarized, binary thinking, the bad-faith arguing, and the torrents of dogma. As I've told many, I think I can provide leadership that is quieter: advice and counsel for those who share our common outlook. This is a vastly different type of leadership than what we in the military are taught and what I tried to exemplify throughout my career, leading from the front. I must say, however, that in certain circumstances, it was my subordinates who showed me their initiative and I was happy to follow. As nineteenth-century French revolutionary Alexandre Auguste Ledru-Rollin is said to have stated: "There go my people; I must follow them because I am their leader."

So, my leadership from the rear starts with this book. I hope that what springs from these pages influences and excites Canadians and provides thoughts that might help people believe in our country and what it can achieve. I still love Canada, but we can do better.

In the space that follows, I'm going to build on my previous remarks and articles and expand on what I think our country is missing. Much of it comes down to leadership and service, two essential elements if our country is to progress and attain its full potential.

I believe Canadians are ready for the changes we need, and our leaders possess the means to effect change directly. Ordinary Canadians, no matter their background, have the power to promote change by the strength of their collective mass. That's democracy. Our leaders must listen and use their authority, influence, and means (financial and otherwise) to turn the will of the people into policy and law. So, let us provide leadership and call our people to service. Let us make service to others and to our country a noble ambition. Let us bring pride and patriotism into the spotlight. Only then can Canada become not only the country it once was, but the country of its immense potential.

I was very lucky to find the career in which I spent almost five decades. I, too, was complacent at first. I did not think I could change the world and did not try. I still don't think I can change it, but as I progressed in rank and experienced a myriad of situations, dangerous or otherwise, I began to feel I needed to make a difference. I'm going to use some of these experiences to illustrate what I learned, and maybe it will awaken something in people reading this book.

One of the people who took the time to write to me after my speech to the Conservative convention, a veteran, questioned my coming out *now* with criticism of the government. He said he had never heard of me during his career and that remarks such as the ones I made in November 2022 and since would have had more weight had I uttered them while in uniform. He even accused me of being a careerist. I am not above reproach and not afraid to be criticized; criticism is the heart of free speech, a principle I spent my career protecting. But I've always thought you can either stay in the machine and try to fix it or get out because you think there is no way to fix it. As far as speaking out while I was in uniform, I accept his comments since he was looking in from the outside. In my time as a colonel and then general officer, the precariousness of the Canadian Armed Forces (CAF) was *never* as bad as I see it now. While in

INTRODUCTION

uniform, my job was to try to influence decisions before they were made, and once the decisions were made, to implement government policy to the best of my ability. I think I was reasonably successful at it and never felt I was rolling over.

What people do not see is the criticism that goes on *within* the military by senior officers who get angry with some of the stupid policies and decisions made by government. We were always told by our public affairs people that if the media want to speak to you, you can speak about your job—what you are doing and what the situation is. Military members are permitted to give facts, but not opinions on policy or socio-political philosophy. In 2023, two admirals walked right up to the edge of that line. One made a video on the current situation in the Royal Canadian Navy, and one gave an interview on the state of the world and Canadians' complacency and comfort. Both officers who spoke out did so based on the realities directly affecting their own jobs. Again, should these two admirals help fix the issues while inside the organization or are they so frustrated that they should leave the service with a splash? They have made the decision to stay and help fix things or at least minimize the impact on their subordinates, but at the same time, they have had the courage to speak out about their job and the current situation. I salute them.

While serving, I always thought one of my responsibilities to my subordinates was to protect them from the sometimes-idiotic decisions of my superiors or at least minimize the impact of these decisions. In the next phase of my career as a senior Department of National Defence executive, I continued to criticize the things I thought were wrong *inside* the machine by speaking directly to those responsible. But now that I'm *outside* the machine and my critics have granted me a platform, I'm going full bore and speaking my mind publicly.

You may not agree with everything in this book, but you'll get a sense of my views as a Canadian who is concerned about our country. Although a lot of this may seem negative, it was the negativity that prompted me to write. I wanted to channel it constructively. I still think this country can achieve greatness with proper leadership and a vision for its people under which they can unite. Leadership is the most important issue facing Canada today and great leaders do exist in our country. I hope this book motivates individual Canadians to care and to demand more of their existing leaders and governments. We all need inspiration. We need to believe that our country is great, and that our country can get better. If this book helps even in a small way, then my objective will have been met.

CHAPTER 1

Becoming

IN 1967, MY FATHER moved our family from St. Jérôme, Quebec, where I was born, to Prince Albert, Saskatchewan. As a result, I went from Grade 8 in French to Grade 9 in English. I'd be lying if I didn't admit that learning English as a fourteen-year-old was traumatic. There was a great deal of teasing on the part of my peers and a lot of angst on my part. After one year, we moved again, this time to Thunder Bay, Ontario, where I completed high school.

My obsession with bilingualism was honed as a teenager. Being able to speak French while attending school in English gave me my first glimpse of the advantages bilingualism provides. Later I saw the challenges of not being bilingual even in my own family, between my younger siblings who had lost much of their French and my older ones who spoke accented English. I would see others experience both the advantages and the challenges throughout my military career, and in most every situation in which I found myself.

My high school guidance counsellor, Mr. Callaghan, had attended the Royal Military College (RMC) in Kingston, Ontario. He had withdrawn before completing the program, but was still a huge supporter of the military and spoke highly of the colleges. I applied to RMC as well as two civilian universities. In those days, going to RMC was advertised as a means of becoming one of Canada's young military executives, complete with the video of a young man in uniform carrying a briefcase. There was no question of fighting for or serving your country.

I was surprised, later in fall 1971, when two visitors from RMC came to my high school to speak to me: the head of the electrical engineering department and a major from the armed forces. This was recruiting of the most personal sort! As luck would have it, the day of the visit, the school was celebrating that 1950s phenomenon known as "Greaser Day," and I was dressed in a sleeveless T-shirt and jeans with my long hair slicked back with Brylcreem. The visitors understood why I was dressed that way and gave me a pass. To be frank, I was probably exactly the kind of young man the CAF was looking for: my grades were in the nineties, I was fit, bilingual, very much involved in school activities, and I had expressed a desire to join the military. My high school graduation photo from the 1972 yearbook is even accompanied by a note saying I hoped to be a general. It was, at the time, the furthest thing from my mind.

In retrospect, we can see more clearly the value of the mentors in our lives. If Mr. Callaghan had not attended RMC and given me encouragement, I would never have considered going there myself. I hadn't even been aware that there were such things as military colleges. Another big influence on me in high school was our shop teacher, Mr. Reszitnyk, who oversaw the Outers Club, dedicated to outdoor activities, such as snowshoeing, canoeing, and camping. I joined along with my best friend, Bryan Harmer, who went on to have an outstanding career as a Canadian National Railway train engineer. Mr. Callaghan and Mr. Reszitnyk were the first of many mentors who guided me through my personal and professional lives. Others were bosses or instructors, while some were colleagues or subordinates. They passed on values and opinions on life, politics, and leadership (good and bad)—all of it contributing to what I am today.

After high school graduation, accompanied by my proud parents, I took a train from Thunder Bay to Winnipeg where I joined the army and was sworn in at the Winnipeg Recruiting Centre. This was my departure from home and the beginning of a career of nearly thirty-five years in uniform.

I became very interested in leadership at RMC and enjoyed the opportunities that came up both during the school year and in my summer military training courses to get a taste of what it's like to lead. I also had fine examples. My first military role model was a fourth-year cadet, Bill Sutherland, our cadet squadron leader. He was always ramrod-straight, with a perfectly fitted uniform and a patrician bearing. I wanted to be just like him.

After my first year of studies, my cohort and I attended the Basic Officer Training Course where one of my instructors was a black sergeant named Cyril Clayton. In him I not only met a role model, but my first true military father figure. I've no doubt many members of my platoon of some thirty officer cadets felt the same about Sgt Clayton. He treated us like "young gentlemen," and it is now obvious to me that he cared so much because those of us who would pass and go on to become officers in the CAF might one day be in command of him and others like him; he wanted us to be the best officers we could be. He was professional, thorough, tough but fair, funny, and so proud to be in the army. He worked hard to make us proud to be in the military also. His was another lesson in leadership.

I was chosen to be Cadet Wing Commander (CWC) in my final year of university, which happened to be the Centennial of RMC; our graduating class will forever be known as the Centennial Class of 1976. As such, I was able to come under the wing of other mentors: the director of cadets, Lieutenant-Colonel Tim Ryley, and the commandant, a WW2 hero of mine, Brigadier-General WW Turner, were gentlemen of impressive bearing and depth who taught me professional lessons that I value to this day. I was riding high as CWC and undoubtedly full of myself, due to the honour the position afforded me. In addition to being featured on a commemorative postage stamp, I met the governor-general, several generals and admirals, and commanded important parades, including one to receive the Freedom of the City of Kingston where I made a huge and humiliating mistake in my parade commands. At another parade I commanded, we were presented new flags by the governor-general on Parliament Hill. I was asked to meet Prime Minister Pierre Trudeau in his office, along with the deputy CWC, Paul Amyotte.

Pierre Trudeau was my mother's idol, and although Trudeaumania was waning, she remained a steadfast fan. I remember Paul and I standing outside his office at the West Block, waiting to go in, with Minister of National Defence James Richardson and the commandant Brigadier General Turner, and saying to myself, "You've come a long way from St. Jérôme and Thunder Bay." The door opened and there stood Trudeau, complete with a rose in his lapel. I conversed with him in both French and English. Later, I received a great photo of Paul, the PM, and me which Trudeau kindly signed with a message in French.

A quick aside on the French language: Quebec is rightly concerned about the erosion of French in the province and in the wider country. As a Quebecer myself, I believe Canada has an advantage over other nations because of its duality of official languages. However, I do not support the idea of making anglophones unwelcome in the province. In fact, I believe Quebec anglophones and anglophones everywhere in Canada are among the most important defenders of the French language. This was always my approach in the CAF: I would tell anglophones that if they ensured a few words of French were spoken every time they presided over a meeting or made remarks, even in the wilds of Alberta, they would reinforce the fact that Canada has two official languages. Too often, I attended meetings and presentations where there was not even an acknowledgement that there might be French speakers in attendance. I'm sure most Canadians are able to say, "*Excusez-moi, je ne parle pas Français, et mes remarques seront en Anglais.*" This is a bit of an obsession of mine: we have two official languages, and we should never appoint officials who cannot speak both languages. And, by the way, a busy official who says they will learn French after being appointed is lying; they will never be able to pick it up with a few lessons a week.

After my last year of academic studies at RMC and what I considered an important "command" position, I had to complete my trade training at Canadian Forces Base Gagetown in New Brunswick as an armoured troop leader. It was there I met another of my mentors, an instructor named Jim Fournier who would be a perfect foil for me. "Jimmy the Axe" knocked me off my perch and kept me humble. He had a reputation for tough, direct, and effective leadership and a deep knowledge and experience in tank tactics. Our course began with sixty-four candidates and ended with only twenty-eight completing the course. Jim's initial troop was fifteen students strong; mid-way through, we were left with five, whom Jim called "the steady five." I came close to failing this course because I thought I could do no wrong. I was brought back to earth with a thump when Fournier told me in front of everyone, "You're not the CWC anymore, so get a grip!" I was shocked and ashamed and resolved to tighten up my leadership principles and approach. It was the end of the beginning of my leadership transition.

A senior non-commissioned officer and the next mentor in my career, Sergeant-Major Ken Maybee, then asked me what my principles of leadership were. I had never thought about it. After some internal reflection, I settled on four that I wrote down and used throughout my career: communications, teamwork, professionalism, and fun. I will provide details of these later.

As my career progressed, I served in Canada, but also on different international missions which gave me a taste of Canada's reputation abroad. My first foreign mission was with the UN in Cyprus in 1977, where I came into contact for the first time with the parties in conflict—Cypriots, Greeks and Turks—as well as soldiers and police of the dozen nations on the peacekeeping team. Later, I spent two years as an exchange officer with the French army, an important milestone in my career as I got to know our French "cousins." To this day, I am a huge Francophile.

I served twice more in Cyprus, then completed two demanding operational missions in Zagreb with the UN and in Kosovo with the Organization for Security and Cooperation in Europe (OSCE). Finally, I served as the first chief of staff of NATO's Supreme Allied Command for Transformation (SACT) in Norfolk, Virginia.

These missions gave me the opportunity to serve with and command international forces, a task at which no one could succeed without finding the common denominator of inclusive leadership. This seemed a natural role for Canada and Canadians. With no sworn enemies, a reputation for tolerance and patience, and a diverse population of proud immigrants, Canada was the perfect nation to provide leaders. These were the days when Canada was seen as a natural peacekeeper, although many do not understand that what made Canada a great *peacekeeping* nation was the *war-fighting* prowess of its military, honed during many conflicts, not least the world wars. Nations looked to us to provide a non-judgmental environment to move past their differences, to work together for a common good, with no fear that we were armed with our own political agenda. In those days, we were brilliant at it. Canada mattered.

This was abundantly clear in Cyprus. Although they are both members of NATO, the Greeks and Turks who divided the island between them had been foes for decades. In my three missions in Cyprus, Canadian peacekeepers could meet with either Greek-Cypriot or Turkish forces and seamlessly bridge the gap, even if armed soldiers from both sides were facing each other across one sandbag-protected street. Armed with this experience, I later ensured officers from Greece and Türkiye could work together in NATO's SACT, putting aside their differences for the common good.

A Canadian peacekeeping force straddled the Golan Heights ceasefire line between Israel and Syria for decades as part of the United Nations Disengagement Observer Force (UNDOF). This was not simple or easy: any national holiday or contingent celebration had to be repeated on both the Israeli and Syrian sides for Canada to avoid being seen as partisan. My wife, who was serving in the mission in 1998–99 as a captain and chief of administration and finance, wistfully pondered the possibility of ever being able to hold these events together, with both Israelis and Syrians in attendance. Her seasoned Israeli Defence Force colleague immediately responded, "That could only ever happen in a Canadian mess."

At the peak of our peacekeeping participation, almost 4,000 Canadians were serving under the UN flag. And today? At the end of October 2023, we were contributing a total of forty-nine peacekeepers. There is no doubt that the era of stable peacekeeping missions such as Cyprus is probably over, but there are other missions in other places in which Canada could participate. Unfortunately, this would require personnel and equipment far above our current dismal levels.

That international reputation that Canada worked so hard to achieve is no longer. Our country is not seen as the world's peacekeeper. Our soldiers and fighters who gave us that reputation would likely shake their heads in disbelief. The ability of the CAF to participate in demanding operational missions is hampered by the lack of personnel, up-to-date equipment, and support from the government and Canadians as a whole. Today, we matter little, and no one seems to care.

CHAPTER 2

Canada's Glorious Past

"The most effective way to destroy people is to deny and obliterate their own understanding of their history"— George Orwell

CANADA HAS AN ILLUSTRIOUS past. Despite all the supposedly progressive apologies for us, despite some episodes in our history when we mistreated some of our citizens, we should look back and be proud of our accomplishments. Two wonderful European countries with different languages, religions, and cultures joined the First Nations to establish our state through trade and collaboration.

There was a time when Canada's reputation was solid. We contributed to the larger world in a myriad of ways, including arts and culture, science and technology, and business and politics. And the contributions were significant. There are historians better able to list our accomplishments, but here are a few.

In WW1, we mobilized 620,000 troops and were victorious at Vimy Ridge, a place of failure for both the French and British. We gave the world Victoria Cross recipient Billy Bishop, one of the greatest fighter pilots of WW1 and, in WW2, the architect of the justifiably famous British Commonwealth Air Training Plan.

We were brave enough to land at Dieppe in WW2 and important enough to earn responsibility for one of the five landing beaches on D-Day. To this day, the combined US–Canada Devil's Brigade, which saw action in Italy and France, remains the template for special forces the world over. Our small country boasted the world's third largest navy at the end of WW2, a force that kept open the vital Atlantic lifeline between North America and Europe. Canada's Elsie McGill, the world's first female aeronautical engineer, the "Queen of the Hurricane" airplane, oversaw the production of over 1,400 fighter aircraft in Thunder Bay during the war.

As mentioned earlier, we became the world's peacekeepers, with 80,000 of us serving during the Cold War. When the world changed on 9/11, Canada stepped up with its allies, serving with distinction in Afghanistan.

We gave the world such authors as Lucy Maud Montgomery, Gabrielle Roy, and Marshall McLuhan, and musicians such as Leonard Cohen, Robert Charlebois, Gordon Lightfoot and Joni Mitchell, among many others. We won two World Series and an NBA title. We beat the Russians on their own ice in 1972. Canada is still the country with the most active NHL players, and we continue to dominate the sport internationally. Even today, forty years after his death, a young man named Terry Fox inspires us all with the unparalleled courage and determination of his Marathon of Hope. We isolated insulin, invented the zipper and the snowblower. We gave the world the Canadarm in space.

Quebec, for all its whining about being obliterated by English culture, has contributed many traditions and customs to Canadian culture. When people are asked to name a distinctly Canadian food, poutine and tourtière often top the list. Montréal is considered the only city in Canada with a truly European flair, and Chef Anthony Bourdain once lamented "without Montréal, Canada would be hopeless."

It would take many books to list all of the individuals and achievements of which our country should be proud. For now, I just want to say a little more about Canada's significant role in world affairs. As small as we are, we had the respect of the international community, and our input was sought by leaders the world over.

In October 1998, I was minding my own business as the director-general of the land staff for Lieutenant General Bill Leach, commander of the army, and Major-General Bruce Jeffries, who was the deputy. The Kosovo crisis was ongoing, with Serbia having reinforced the province with many units of the Yugoslav National Army and ministry of the interior police to control the Albanian majority.

American ambassador Dick Holbrooke had managed to talk Serbia's leader Slobodan Milosevic into signing an agreement to reduce Serb military and police forces in Kosovo and to calm tensions until a political agreement could be reached on the status of the province. Holbrooke also managed to convince the Organization for Security and Co-operation in Europe to put together an unarmed civilian mission of about 2,000 staff to "verify" the agreement (reduction of forces, upholding human rights, etc.). This was to be the Kosovo Verification Mission (KVM). The OSCE, an alliance of fifty-four countries at the time, had never put together such a large mission—its experience stemmed mostly from election monitoring.

When the OSCE–Serbia agreement was signed in October 1998, the UK sent Major-General Karol Drewienkiewicz (known as MGen DZ) to OSCE headquarters in Vienna with a small planning team to put together the mission. When DZ was needed in Kosovo to set up the mission on the ground, the UK made an urgent request to Canada to provide a backup for him as head of the KVM support unit. We were asked because we had a reputation for good staff officers who were not afraid to act. Somehow my name came up, and I was asked to deploy for "up to six weeks" in Vienna, until things stabilized, and the mission could continue running.

I received the order and quickly started my preparations, deploying with civilian clothes only and jumping on an aircraft to Vienna in the middle of November. When I arrived in the Austrian capital, it quickly became apparent to me that we were starting the mission with a blank sheet of paper. We were organizing everything from scratch: getting nations to provide people, setting up the structure, and buying vehicles and equipment on the free market. I remember evaluating bids from different vehicle companies (in particular, Land Rover and Jeep) to provide armoured 4x4s for the mission. We looked over the bids, their cost, and other specifications, and I made the decision to go with Jeep. (The Land Rover bid was much more expensive, but having owned two Land Rovers since, I think I might have made the wrong decision.)

After a few days in Vienna, I became friendly with some of the defence attachés in Vienna, many of whom were attachés to Austria, but accredited to the OSCE. One, the UK attaché, was a typical Brit. Although he was a military officer, the first time he came to my office, he was dressed in civilian clothes. His hair was down below his collar. He was wearing the usual blue-and-white striped shirt, a pin-striped dark suit, red suspenders, and bright red socks. A few days later, we were out for lunch, and he mentioned to me that he had heard that nominations for the heads of the Regional Centres (RCs) in Kosovo (based on the five geographic districts in the province at the time) would be appointed soon, starting with the Prizren district just across from Albania. He noted that the Kosovo Contact Group nations (the US, UK, France, Germany, and Russia) would not provide the heads of RCs, but that they would come from nations he dismissively called "minions," meaning lesser nations. Some days later, the head of mission, US Ambassador William Walker, who was already deployed in Kosovo, asked Canada to send *me* as the first head of RC in Prizren. As soon as my name was announced, I received a bottle of champagne from the UK attaché with a note of apology. He should have known that Canada was not a minion. Its leadership was valued, even if it wasn't a member of the Contact Group.

Here's another illustration of the international weight Canada wielded at that time. Several nations had already deployed unarmed groups, the so-called Kosovo Diplomatic Observer Missions (KDOMs), which were based on bilateral arrangements with Kosovo and did not come under the OSCE umbrella. These KDOMs had been operating on the ground for some weeks and days. The two biggest were British and American, each with a few dozen vehicles and scores of personnel who patrolled in Kosovo and reported to their nations through foreign ministry channels. To its credit, Canada also deployed a KDOM. We mattered on the world stage and along with the UK, the US, and other G7 nations, we had a seat at the table and the international weight to make a difference in the cause of peace.

MGen DZ had meanwhile been deployed to Kosovo's capital, Pristina, to begin setting up the KVM headquarters. The headquarters was to have a head of mission, Ambassador Walker, and five deputy heads of mission allocated to each of the nations of the Kosovo Contact Group. In March 1999, the KVM was evacuated from Kosovo because there was a threat that the Serbian authorities directed by Milosevic might take its personnel hostage. I was then asked to organize and take command of a task force to assist Albania with the influx of refugees Milosevic was pushing out of Kosovo. My service in the KVM in Kosovo and Albania was undoubtedly the most difficult in my career, but I believe that we made a difference in the lives of the people of the region and that Canada shone brightly through that service. It was my honour to be recognized by the governor-general with the Meritorious Service Cross for my performance in that mission.

On September 11, 2001, I was serving as the assistant deputy chief of the defence staff (DCDS) as a major-general. The DCDS at that time, Vice-Admiral Greg Maddison, was the overall coordinator of all domestic and international missions on behalf of the chief of defence staff. As his assistant, my job was to act in his absence, and also manage the development of innovative operational solutions for the CAF. The role, in effect, was to transform CAF operations. As soon as the terrible events of that morning began to unfold, all of us gathered in the operations rooms of National Defence headquarters (NDHQ) to decide on the actions that needed to be taken.

The seriousness of that day, the terror of what had happened, and the fear of what could still happen was written on the faces of the senior leaders in the room. In coordination with Transport Canada and North American Aerospace Defense Command (NORAD), the Canadian airspace was closed and all flights then in the air were to be landed at the nearest airports. In total, 239 flights carrying 33,000 passengers were diverted to Gander, Newfoundland, that day with the aim of avoiding large urban centres and other potential targets. Militaries around the globe scrambled to plan for any and every "what if" situation. Everyone was looking to government leaders for information, comfort, and reassurance. Some leaders were born that day, and some were obviously out of their league. When the towers collapsed, so, too, did the stability that we all had enjoyed for decades.

The events set in motion by Osama bin Laden caused me to believe that our world was about to change drastically. I believe that was one of his major objectives and that he was successful on that day. No longer would anyone feel completely safe in any situation. Billions of dollars would be spent on new security arrangements for travel, immigration, and protection of vital infrastructure. We began to live our lives looking over one shoulder. The comparative peace and world order that came post WW2, boosted by the fall of the USSR, disappeared when Mohammed Atta flew American Airlines Flight 11 into the North Tower of the World Trade Center. Life would be different going forward. How would we deal with this new threat?

Less than a century ago, our forefathers faced the forces of evil in a war that was truly global in nature. Theirs was a struggle they could not afford to lose. Now the fight had once again been brought to us, a war against terror that would involve all populations, even those living in dictatorships (remember Iran being bombed by ISIS in January 2024?). The stakes were such for our generation that we could never return to a state of relative security without defeating or at least degrading the scourge of terrorism. This was a threat against all societies, liberal and otherwise: it was—is—*our* generation's world war.

The problem we faced was how to defeat the threat. Was that even possible? Or could we only reduce it and minimize the chances of terrorist actions? Unlike wars of olden days, the enemies weren't clad in military uniforms. They wore the clothes of civilians and hid in busy cities. There was no designated battlefield. Our opponents didn't have tanks of their own but could blow ours to smithereens with improvised explosive devices (IEDs). They didn't have an air force but trained to hijack civilian planes to destroy infrastructure, kill innocent people, and devastate the morale of those watching it unfold. They used women and children as shields. Their suicide bombers were heralded as martyrs. They were so thoroughly indoctrinated in their cause that they were willing to opportunistically engage our forces and then hide in plain sight, waiting as long as it took to re-start this cycle. It was clear they would never give up. We needed to get ahead of them, to find a way to recognize and defeat the threat before it struck. As a result, we engaged in major efforts to conduct surveillance, monitor social media, exchange information on terrorist cells, and take direct action to prevent incidents and attacks. It was the only way, in the words of David Frum, to "restore deterrence."

Much of this was novel at the time, although it has become less so over time. No nation declares war on another anymore. In WW2, the Canadian parliament officially declared war on Germany on September 10, 1939. Since then, even during the Korean conflict, Canada has not declared war on another nation. Most nations don't. Even Russian president Vladimir Putin did not call his invasion of Ukraine in 2022 a war, but a "special military operation." In 2001, George W. Bush and most Americans used the term "war on terror," but in Canada, we were directed to use "campaign against terrorism," which reflected our less-warlike approach. Canadians wanted to show that they were different from the Americans, who were perceived by some as warmongers. In any case, Canada was in the crucible now and we needed to do something.

To show you how Canada mattered at that time, a few weeks after 9/11, we were asked to send a delegation to the Tampa, Florida, headquarters of US Central Command to coordinate what Canada might be able to provide for the campaign against terrorism. CENTCOM, at that time, was the geographic area that encompassed Afghanistan and the Middle East. I was tasked to lead the delegation, with an RCAF brigadier-general and an RCN commodore to assist me. In Tampa, we were met at MacDill Air Force Base by Lieutenant-General Michael (Rifle) Delong, USMC, the deputy commander of CENTCOM. I was whisked directly to meet the commander, General Tommy Franks, and we discussed the general situation while smoking cigars.

Our delegation was provided with offices, phones, and computers. Through discussions with NDHQ and our American colleagues, we looked into what military "packages" the US could use and what Canada could commit. We were immediately integrated into the US headquarters as allies and friends. I remember that the first offer Canada made was to reassign the Canadian ship serving with the NATO Standing Naval Force Atlantic to the US-led coalition. That coalition soon became known as "Coalition of the Willing" and eventually counted dozens of nations.

Every day, Franks held a briefing and update at 9 a.m. in a conference room with a U-shaped table. At the bottom of the U sat Franks, with a sign to his right that said "Canada" where I would sit, one on the left that said "UK," and further left "Australia." Our three nations were the first to arrive in Tampa to join the coalition and obviously were those the US was counting on to assist in the war against terrorism. Continuing down the length of each side of the table were the US two-star generals or flag officers who were heads of different sections of the headquarters such as Operations, Intelligence, Personnel. On the screen connected by secure video-teleconference were the different subordinate commanders deployed in the region near Afghanistan: the commander of the naval component, the land force commander, the air component commander, special forces, and others.

Each day at this conference, the participants would enter the room early and then stand when Franks would walk in right on the hour. Then, he would go through the briefings on the intelligence situation, the operations, status of forces, and so on. He would ask questions and provide feedback so that he could keep the American president informed as required. In the US, commanders such as Franks reported directly to President George W. Bush. I can't help but contrast this to Canada, where politicians such as the minister of National Defence make operational announcements, often with the chief of defence staff not even present.

So here was Canada at the right hand of the US in the coalition of the willing. We had been told there would be no 9 a.m. meeting on Sunday, October 7 because General Franks was giving his staff some time off.[1] However, a young soldier came into our office early Sunday morning to announce that there was a change of plans and that the commander had decided to hold a meeting after all. I rushed in. The group was much more sombre than usual. On the screen were not only the deployed commanders but also US secretary of defense Donald Rumsfeld, logging in from the White House. Franks walked in and took his spot. His first words were ". . . at noon today our time, the first Tomahawk Land Attack Missile will fall on Kabul." It was a historic moment that would launch a conflict in which more than 150 Canadians would lose their lives and many more would be injured.

Franks went around the room and then out to the deployed commanders to see if there were any last-minute issues that might cause us to abort the mission. There were none. Rumsfeld spoke and on behalf of the president, who had wanted to be present but was otherwise occupied, explained this was an important moment that marked the start of the US

---

[1] There were meetings at 9 a.m. everyday since our arrival, and at the meeting on October 6, a Saturday, Franks walked in wearing shorts, a Hawaiian shirt, and sandals. He recounted how the staff had been working flat-out since 9/11 and that he was trying to tell them to relax for a few hours. We were told there would be no meeting the next day, a Sunday, so with my two colleagues we decided that we would come in in civilian clothes. I wanted to attend church, if possible, then perhaps do a bit of work and maybe some sightseeing. Unfortunately, as the account above relates, this was the day the conflict began and there I was sat at the right of Franks in my Hawaiian shirt and chinos while he and everyone else were in full combat uniform. The next day, I was of course back in uniform and Franks punched me in the arm when he came in, saying, "I liked you better the way you were dressed yesterday."

and its allies' retaliation for the lives lost in the attacks of 9/11. Aware of the importance of the moment, I immediately called our chief of defence staff, General Ray Henault, to let him know the countdown had begun. He later told me he had reached Prime Minister Jean Chrétien, who thanked him for the information and now understood why President Bush wanted to speak to him at 11 a.m.

Canada mattered and was an important ally.

Later, I will tell a story of our influence in NATO when the organization moved into the twenty-first century with a new command—NATO Transformation Command, the only NATO HQ outside Europe—and Canada was called upon to provide the first chief of staff of that command (me), responsible for organizing and creating the headquarters in Norfolk, Virginia, in 2003. Another example of how Canada mattered.

Later, Canadian Major-General Walter Natynczyk was appointed deputy commander of the US Army's III Corps at Fort Hood (now Fort Cavazos) in Texas. The corps consisted of 35,000 troops in ten brigades. Natynczyk deployed with them to Iraq where he participated in Operation Iraqi Freedom. The Americans rarely let foreigners lead their troops. Canadians have been the exception, especially in Afghanistan and Iraq. Natynczyk was later awarded the Meritorious Service Cross specifically for his efforts in that operation. As well as Natynczyk in Iraq, another Canadian general, David Fraser, had American units under command during Operation Medusa in Afghanistan in 2006. He led the transition from the US Operation Enduring Freedom to the NATO–ISAF coalition. Canada was entrusted as the lead nation for this operation and received many international accolades for the results, which owed a lot to Fraser's leadership, skill, diplomacy, and experience. He, too, was awarded the Meritorious Service Cross for his efforts and was named the 2006 Vimy Award laureate.

Canada was sought out for its participation in these crucial missions through the world wars to twenty-first-century conflicts. Our contributions, regardless of size, were valued. We were successful at them. We mattered. What happened?

CHAPTER 3

Canada Exits the World's Stage

INTERNATIONALLY, CANADA IS FALTERING. We no longer have a place on the world stage. We are ignored or dismissed by our allies. We do not pay our way in the international arena. We are not taken seriously. Recently, the editorial board of the *Wall Street Journal* told Canada to sit at the kids' table, and we were excoriated by a US senator for not pulling our weight in NORAD. The simple fact is that "Canada's standing in the world is directly proportionate to how America perceives us. Other countries take us seriously when they see America take us seriously," said Goldy Hyder, president of the Business Council of Canada, lamenting our country being left out of the latest development in the Indo-Pacific region. If our closest ally and best friend dismisses us, what will the rest of the world do?

I think Canadians have inflated ideas of how we are perceived internationally, believing that our place has not changed in the past few years. We have been brainwashed since 2015 to think that a prime minister's looks and coloured socks can make *us* look great. Canadians seem not to care what the military needs, nor how the CAF can project our image and our values across the world. They have been convinced by the media and the government to see the CAF as an old white force riddled with sexual predators, one that really isn't necessary except in cases of domestic emergencies such as floods or wildfires. Canadians also ignorantly believe that we are safe, completely safe. We have no enemies, everybody loves us, nobody would ever attack us, and regardless of how much we let down the US, it will *always* protect us. Canada needs to wake up to the fact that we have a role to play—that's what allies and neighbours do for each other—and that in this world, we are *not* safe.

One way to gauge Canada's status on the world stage is through our military exchanges. Canada, with its two official languages and French–English duality, is able to span the gulf of Anglo-Saxon countries as well as those belonging to *La Francophonie*. I was fortunate to be chosen as the Canadian exchange officer to a French regiment in the late 1970s. The French army was composed of conscripts at that time, citizens who were brought into the army to serve for a year. The French system worked very well, and these conscripts (*appelés*), young men from every part of France, were trained and focused on defending their country against the USSR-led Warsaw Pact. I have many great memories of commanding two troops of French conscript soldiers for a total of more than fourteen months.

The French army expected the troop leader to take soldiers who had completed a month of basic training and one or two months of specialist training (driver, or gunner, for example) and bring them up to a standard that would enable them to fight as an operational unit. The French unit I belonged to was stationed in Sedan, in the Ardennes alongside the Belgian border. The *12e Régiment de Chasseurs* was later disbanded when France abandoned conscription. When I served there, however, the regiment was more than a thousand strong and I felt I could take my troop of twenty-one soldiers and hold our own against the Soviets.

The French officers treated me as one of their own, and I believe my soldiers were proud and felt special to have a Canadian officer as their troop leader. Each one of our troop garages had a crest identifying the specific troop by the name of the leader. One night, my soldiers took the crest down and painted a red maple leaf under my name and replaced it above the garage door. To this day, I wish I had brought that crest back to Canada.

In those days, Canada was still recognized as an important ally by France, and military exchanges were one practical manifestation of that recognition. My service with the French remained a constant in my later career, as I would meet French military colleagues, now often friends, in different missions abroad; there was an immediate connection and respect because of these early relationships. During my mission in the former Yugoslavia as a colonel with the UN Protection Force (UNPROFOR) in the mid-1990s, I reconnected with Dominique Trinquand, who was my best friend when both of us were lieutenants in Sedan. Eventually, as a major-general, I co-chaired the Franco-Canadian Military Cooperation Committee with a French colleague, Amiral Alain Coldefy. The world is small and the military world even smaller. My service and connection to France was later recognized when I was awarded the French *Légion d'Honneur* in the rank of officer.

Canada mattered and our ability to this day to connect with two great cultures gives us an advantage few possess. We are squandering it.

The president and CEO of the Canadian Chamber of Commerce, Perrin Beatty, sent the prime minister an open letter in 2023 decrying the woeful state of Canada's influence on the world stage. His letter was not the first public plea, addressed to Canadians in general and the government in particular, to pop our bubble of complacency and awaken us to how the world has changed. The relative peace we have enjoyed since the end of the Cold War has never been as challenged as it is today. And Canada, once a strong nation and a player on the world stage, has no role in shaping the future. It is past time to understand the importance of the relationship between the capabilities of the military and our diplomatic weight internationally, and to do something about it.

In 2023, the commander of the Royal Canadian Navy released a video explaining to his sailors the dire state of the service. He spoke of how new ships were on the horizon, but not for many years. He encouraged his sailors to keep working hard even in the face of current personnel and equipment challenges. It was a necessary action by a leader, explaining the unvarnished truth of the situation, including the time it would take for the navy to redress the issues. I am sure the Privy Council Office, the prime minister's personal support department, was unhappy with the video. I'm not sure the commander had asked for or received approval for release of the video before putting it online, but I am sure the sailors thought, "finally, one of our senior leaders is telling it like it is."

A few days after the video's release, the commander of Canadian Joint Operations Command (CJOC) was quoted in an interview also telling it like it is: Canadians are "overly comfortable" in spite of the deteriorating international situation. The CJOC commands and coordinates all military operations in Canada and abroad, so its commander is uniquely aware of all the hotspots in the world and the potential for regional conflicts to escalate into broader war. Again, I'm not sure his comments were pre-approved, but he spoke to the current situation as he knows it, and I am glad he did. Our serving CAF personnel are doing an amazing job with very little in terms of funding, equipment, training, and government support. They are the best at this, but they are tired. It is difficult to imagine them being stretched further and perhaps being in harm's way, but the current global situation may require it.

There are bigger issues. The aforementioned Perrin Beatty was minister of National Defence when a 1987 defence white paper proposed a rearming of the CAF, increased funding, and—don't roll your eyes—the acquisition of nuclear submarines. The whole submarine issue is for another day, although I will say his idea was good then and it is good now.

Our global diplomatic muscle has been allowed to atrophy. At Global Affairs Canada, our diplomats are probably feeling as downtrodden as the military. We hear that there has been a complete stop to language courses for diplomats about to travel to their foreign postings due to a lack of funding. Canada's foreign service officers were envied by their international peers because we would ensure they had a functional knowledge of the language of the country of their posting. This will no longer be the case. How ridiculous.

Missteps internationally are a symptom of decline. First, our PM travelled to India with his family and tried to look more Indian than the Indians themselves. Then, he announced in the House of Commons that India was behind the murder of a Sikh separatist in Canada, provoking a debacle that brought a diplomatic maelstrom. Although the information is apparently corroborated by the "five-eyes" intelligence community, no evidence was released. Whether there is proof or not, you do not announce this in the House of Commons without having your ducks in a row unless you are merely trying to ensure the Sikh vote goes your way in the next election. We heard in May 2024 that the RCMP had finally brought charges against three individuals from Edmonton.

Canada was excluded from the Quadrilateral Security Dialogue, known as the QUAD, between India, Japan, Australia, and the United States. As a large Pacific nation with an Indo-Pacific strategy, we ought to have been part of this group of influential countries.

Evidence of Chinese interference in our elections and in the lives of Chinese Canadians, not to mention the existence of "Chinese Police Stations" on Canadian soil, forced the government to set up one more inquiry. The "rapporteur," a decent, humble former governor-general, David Johnston, embarrassed himself and us all with his weak report. He ended up resigning. In response to strong pressure on the government, a commission of inquiry was finally struck to investigate foreign interference.

When Russia invaded Ukraine in 2022, Europe was caught in a trap. Members of the EU wanted to support Ukraine and levy sanctions on Russia, but needed a way to replace the crucial Russian gas they were being supplied. Other gas-producing nations were approached, including Canada, but we were unable to help since Ottawa has created obstacles for our gas producers that impair their ability to bring their supply to market. To make matters worse, our prime minister told the visiting chancellor of Germany that there is "no business case" to provide natural gas. Now, I am not an economist, nor a gas executive, but I would think there *is* actually a business case for Canada to build a pipeline from our gas fields to both coasts so that new terminals can export this important and relatively clean resource. The US has managed in recent years to become the world's largest exporter of natural gas, with almost $100 billion in revenue and thousands of jobs added to its economy.

In January 2023, the Canadian government promised a $400 million National Advanced Surface-to-Air Missile System to protect Ukraine's skies. Photo ops and fanfare accompanied the announcement and prompted a heartfelt thank-you from President Zelenskyy. Three months later, Defence Minister Anita Anand declared the coveted system was "en route" to Ukraine. She lied. As of February 2024, it has not been delivered and there is no indication of when, or if, it ever will be delivered.

Then there was the flip-flop of statements on the unprovoked Hamas terrorist attack on Israel in October 2023. We abandoned Israel, our traditional friend and staunch ally. While we were being publicly rebuked by Prime Minister Netanyahu for our lack of moral clarity, we were being thanked by the leader of Hamas, a designated terrorist organization. Our leaders seem to think Canada can have it both ways: endorse Israel's right to defend itself, but call for an immediate ceasefire, all while refusing to condemn the hatred expressed in daily protests on our streets. That hypocrisy might save a few votes, but it makes Canada and its prime minister look weak and ignorant.

All this has harmed Canada's relationships with its usual partners. The US rarely consults with us anymore. Even when they do consult, we don't want to play. In former days, as I illustrated above, Canada was seen as a reliable ally. Even if we did not contribute much militarily, our support was important morally.

AUKUS (the security pact between Australia, the United Kingdom, and the United States) was signed on September 15, 2021. If Trudeau had been asked to join AUKUS, I'm sure he would have declined. He implied as much when he dismissed a potential Canadian role in AUKUS saying, "This is a deal for nuclear submarines, which Canada is not currently or any time soon in the market for. Australia is." To the government's credit, it then went on to publish its Indo-Pacific strategy, but how could we let the opportunity pass to collaborate with Australia, the US, and the UK to protect our interests in the vast geographic area that abuts our western coast? Trudeau seemed to minimize the scope of AUKUS, limiting it to nuclear submarine technology. That is Pillar 1 of the agreement. Pillar 2 states that "Australia, the United Kingdom, and the United States will develop and field joint advanced military capabilities to promote security and stability in the Indo-Pacific region." It involves technology for defence, tracking and intelligence. Japan and New Zealand have expressed interest in joining Pillar 2, all the more reason why we, too, should be part of AUKUS. (At the time of writing, there seems to be an effort by Canada to join pillar 2 of AUKUS.)

Now, we do not even get asked to participate in international alliances. In May 2022, President Biden launched the Indo-Pacific Economic Framework. Canada was not included. Since then, our government has asked to join, probably realizing that when you are left off the team, you are missing out on economic and trade opportunities.

We also seem uninterested in anticipating future events. The US election this year may well be won by Donald Trump in his sequel as president. European nations are already preparing for that eventuality, particularly where NATO funding is concerned. During Trump's presidency, he had chastised complacent nations such as Canada for not reaching the agreed-upon goal of at least 2 percent of GDP on defence spending. If he should win, he is likely to have the same attitude, even to the potential of challenging NATO's Article 5, the "one for all and all for one" concept, opting out of collective defence. European nations have begun to think of assuming more of their own defence responsibilities instead of relying entirely on the protection provided by US military might. Canada ought to do the same.

Even with a well-considered strategy in place, you can't act on it if you can't support it. We had three naval vessels in the Pacific in 2023 because of our new Indo-Pacific strategy. Good. We showed our flag. These ships then returned home. Why? There are not enough sailors for the few ships we have, and many of those ships need refits with no chance of new replacement vessels anytime soon. In effect, the hands of the chief of defence staff are tied. He/she is unable to continue to show the flag in Asia to support our diplomats. There will be no Canadian presence, no port visits to our Pacific peers. Sorry Australia, we wish we could exercise with you as part of AUKUS, but we are not part of it. And, sorry, United States, although we have a senior officer in the headquarters of Indo-Pacific Command, that is apparently where our field commitment ends.

We owe thanks to Perrin Beatty for pointing out that our neglect of the CAF has repercussions far beyond military issues. And to General Eyre, Vice-Admiral Topshee, and Vice-Admiral Auchterlonie for speaking out and telling us the truth about our forces. A capable CAF can help our reputation abroad and provide Canadians with faith that our country is once again a nation that matters. Perhaps it's time to ditch the fancy socks and photo ops and begin to contribute to a stable world order that is critical to our future.

***

My Ukrainian father-in-law was a survivor of two of the twentieth century's greatest cataclysms: the Holodomor and WW2. He witnessed horrific injustices. He was also a huge believer in the UN. I once asked him why, and he responded, "If we do not have the UN, who do we have?" I would argue that with the current moral corruption of the institution, we are well on the way to having nothing. It is being run by a climate alarmist, UN secretary-general António Guterres, who was consumed by the imbecility of his organization's climate change conference, COP28, in Dubai last year.

On the Hamas–Israel war, the fact that a ceasefire existed before the attack by Hamas on October 7, 2023, has largely been forgotten by the UN and a large number of countries. On December 12, 2023, the UN General Assembly approved a resolution demanding an immediate "humanitarian ceasefire" without mentioning Hamas terrorists. Canada voted in favour. The text at the bottom of the resolution is shocking: "The resolution does not condemn Hamas or make any specific reference to the extremist group." Note the word "extremist" and not "terrorist." How could this resolution pass, and with Canadian support, no less?

In the early months of 2024, the United Nations Relief and Works Agency for Palestinian Refugees in the Near East (UNRWA) was shown to be completely at odds with its stated aim to help Palestinian refugees. Astonishingly, in its seven decades of existence, UNRWA has not resettled one Palestinian refugee. It seemingly has no mission other than to foster hatred of Jews and the state of Israel and to support Hamas. The evidence is both overt and covert: overt in the Gaza school textbooks and curricula, which promote Jew hate and the benefits of martyrdom, and covert in that UNRWA staffers actually participating in the genocidal Operation Al-Aqsa Flood that took place on October 7. UNRWA has insisted the textbooks have been removed and its 7/10 terrorists fired. But we have only UNRWA's word for that, and many of its donors are suspending or pausing funding to the organization. That this blatant hatred was allowed until it was revealed, not by UNRWA, but by Israel and the NGO UN Watch, should make a convincing argument that this organization needs to be dismantled. The murderers should have been brought to justice, not simply fired.

In the aftermath of the WW2, the United Nations High Commission for Refugees (UNHCR) had its hands full with millions of European refugees to resettle. In the years that followed, wars and uprisings resulted in many more refugees in need of resettlement. A million Jews were expelled from Arab countries following the creation of the state of Israel. Those Jews—in fact, any and all European Jews who so desired—were settled without UN assistance in Israel. Other refugees sought help from the UN, too. Terry Glavin in the *National Post* on January 31, 2024, summed up the numbers as follows: "Roughly 14 million Muslims and Hindus were uprooted and resettled on the Indian subcontinent. Ten million ethnic Germans were driven out of Eastern Europe after WW2, eventually finding a home in West Germany. A million North Vietnamese settled in South Vietnam in the 1950s, 600,000 Chinese fled to Hong Kong after Mao's triumph in 1949, and three million Koreans fled the north to settle in South Korea during the early 1950s." The UNHCR and the other temporary UN agencies created to manage the movement of these refugees did just that. Afterward, they were dismantled. Mission accomplished. But UNRWA has no intention of resettling the Palestinians; instead, it encourages them to remain refugees, it grants that status to all continuing generations so that the initial 700,000 Palestinians displaced in the wake of Israel's creation now number over 5 million. How is this helping? How can a UN organization discourage resettlement while encouraging life in permanent refugee camps where its own staff teach violent revolution, Jew hatred, and martyrdom? And how can the UN renew the UNRWA mandate every three years since 1949 without requiring accountability?

The ceasefire resolution and the exposure of UNRWA's support for Hamas have demonstrated the UN is a corrupt and now virtually useless institution. Sadly, Canada aided and abetted the global organization's lack of moral courage.

My experience with the United Nations spans some twenty-six months in total, in missions abroad in 1977, 1983, 1990, and 1993. As the acting chief of staff for joint operations for Canada in 1998, I oversaw and coordinated all international missions and domestic operations. These included all UN missions in which Canada participated. Senior Canadian commanders employed by the UN in foreign peace missions such as Major-General (ret.) Lewis MacKenzie and Lieutenant-General (ret.) Roméo Dallaire have written or spoken of their experiences; many of these were extremely negative and speak of an institution that is bloated, politicized, ineffective, and unreactive. In my former life, I was not as harsh towards the UN. Yes, my experience supported the fact that the UN is a bloated bureaucracy that is sometimes unable to make decisions quickly. But I always had the feeling UN bureaucrats were serving an institution that they believed in, for the good of humanity. Until now.

It is certainly true that the UN had to work hard to support the different missions it coordinated. When I arrived as the chief operations officer (COO) of UNPROFOR in Zagreb, Croatia, in 1993, the mission put me in charge of the coordination of the six subordinate commands totalling about 30,000 multinational troops. This is almost equivalent to a corps-level structure with subordinate divisions. Such a structure required a large operations centre to keep track of operations to enable the command to deal with transgressions like ceasefire violations, ethnic cleansing, belligerent firefights, illegal checkpoints, and illegal confiscation of humanitarian aid. There was a need to report these incidents to senior commanders and also to the situation room at UN headquarters in New York.

At the time of my arrival in March 1993, the UNPROFOR Operations Centre was a small room about the size of a broom closet with a desk, a phone, and a map on the wall. A lone duty officer manned the phone 24/7 and any incident in the field was reported to him. He then passed on that information to the subordinate commands and informed New York by telephone, not the most effective approach. Sadly, the same was true of UN headquarters. As Lewis MacKenzie wrote and said years earlier, UN headquarters was inefficient in operational terms.

We set about enlarging the operations centre in Zagreb with a number of desks where officers assigned to each subordinate commands could get detailed reports from the field and mark a large map of the area of operations. The force commander and the senior staff would receive a briefing from me in the operations centre every morning on the events of the past twenty-four hours. He would provide his direction and guidance. At the same time, UN headquarters was setting up its own situation room in New York and we were able to communicate better. Nevertheless, it seemed the media was always one step ahead of us, and CNN, SkyNews, and BBC sometimes had the information on events before we could bring it up the chain of command. But at least we were able to develop a good relationship with New York, which helped me regain some trust in the UN.

In 1999, I returned from the Kosovo Verification Mission. Louise Fréchette, a former deputy minister of National Defence with whom I had worked during my time at NDHQ, was serving as the first deputy secretary-general of the UN under Secretary-General Kofi Annan. She contacted the HQ and asked if I would be available to come to New York to help plan a future UN mission in Kosovo. It was an incredible opportunity to see the big machine up close. What I remember from the two weeks I spent there is the desire of the staff to do good and to make a difference. I had met and sat in on meetings with Kofi Annan (who was head of the department of peacekeeping on my visit to UN HQ in 1993) and I developed huge respect for the man, respect that only grew when he was appointed secretary-general and worked hard to reform the bureaucracy. Appointing Fréchette as deputy was a stroke of genius. Her no-nonsense approach was much needed, even if she struggled to pare the fat.

There are still places where the UN can be effective. I had the opportunity to testify at the International Criminal Tribunal for the Former Yugoslavia (ICTY) in The Hague on three occasions. The ICTY was a UN court of law that dealt with war crimes that took place during the conflicts in the Balkans in the 1990s. Testimony in court is a natural consequence of service in international missions—in my case, in the former Yugoslavia on two occasions: once with UNPROFOR and once with the OSCE KVM. In all three cases when I testified at the Hague, it was voluntary and I was a witness for the prosecution. I saw it as a way to get closure for some of the difficult experiences I had lived through during the missions. My first appearance was to testify against Slobodan Milosevic and then twice more against some of his subordinates.

For Milosevic, the prosecution asked me questions for about ninety minutes, then it was Milosevic's turn. He was defending himself. His first question accused me of being an agent of NATO while deployed in Yugoslavia. Of course, I was with the UN and then the OSCE, so I responded that I was not. I wonder what he would have said when I later became the chief of staff of NATO's Supreme Allied Command Atlantic then of Transformation. I had finally become a true agent of NATO!

Sadly, Milosevic died of a heart attack in his cell before the trial concluded. My sense after returning from Kosovo was that he was truly in the same mould as Hitler, and I said so to Minister of Defence McCallum. Even so, it was clear the UN was the only body that could set up a court system to bring perpetrators of inhuman actions to justice. It did the same with the Rwandan genocide in 1994. But now with its relentless focus on climate change and support of a recognized terror organization, Hamas, it has lost credibility with me.

* * *

Canada's influence in NATO, which celebrates its seventy-fifth anniversary in 2024, was initially huge; Canada was one of its twelve founding nations in 1949. Influence in NATO, however, is commensurate with the contributions a country provides. Today, because of our meagre funding, our weakened CAF, and our reduced diplomatic clout, Canada has lost much of its influence and prestige.

NATO's principle of "an attack on one is an attack on all" appealed to many nations beyond the twelve founders and its membership continues to grow with Finland and Sweden joining recently after the Russian invasion of Ukraine. NATO was originally formed as a defensive alliance in the aftermath of WW2. A few years later, the Soviet Union formed its own version of NATO, the Warsaw Pact, and the two bodies essentially defined the major players in the Cold War. NATO's plans were, and are, still defensive in nature. After the fall of the Berlin Wall in 1989, the USSR dissolved into its constituent republics along with the Warsaw Pact and the raison d'être of NATO came into question. Soon, NATO attempted to establish closer relations with Russia and Ukraine independently, creating the NATO–Russia Council and the NATO–Ukraine Council. A means of collaboration with former Soviet republics was also created; it was called the Partnership for Peace process, which nations could join with the goal of eventual full membership in NATO. From its sixteen members when the USSR was dissolved, NATO has grown to thirty-two nations, including Finland and Sweden. The fact that these two countries, which remained neutral throughout the Cold War, are now in NATO is a crucial indicator that the security situation has deteriorated.

The strength of NATO lies in its role as a permanent institutional mechanism of dialogue on global issues among like-minded nations. The North Atlantic Council, made up of representatives of all thirty-two nations who reside in Brussels at the ambassador level, meets regularly: that is the *political* level of NATO. Each nation provides a permanent military representative of general or admiral rank in Brussels, and they also meet regularly as the NATO Military Committee: that is the *military* level of NATO.

One thing we often forget is the tactical importance of NATO which involves the less sexy stuff, like standardization of techniques, tactics, and procedures, as well as kit and ammunition for interoperability. You can imagine the chaos if rifles or howitzers from different nations used different calibres of ammunition. Standardization allows forces from different nations to arrive prepared to plug in easily and be ready to exercise or operate seamlessly. Different levels of HQs exist and are ready to undertake operations once forces are activated. Yes, they are more ponderous than national headquarters because they are multinational, but they still exist and don't have to be sourced after a crisis.

In 1952, NATO created the Supreme Allied Commander Atlantic (SACLANT) with the operational mission to command all NATO forces in the Atlantic area, including Canada and the US. This mostly naval command was based in Norfolk, Virginia. The command group consisted of three senior officers by the early 2000s: the commander was an American four-star admiral; the deputy SACLANT was a UK Royal Navy four-star admiral; and the chief of staff was a Royal Canadian Navy three-star admiral. The only other Supreme Headquarters and Commander in NATO at that time was Supreme Allied Commander Europe (SACEUR), traditionally a four-star American, the first of which was Dwight D. Eisenhower.

One interesting fact is that SACLANT HQ was the only NATO HQ outside Europe. Manned by officers and sailors from all NATO nations, this large HQ in the middle of Virginia, on the largest naval base in the world, was *the* trans-Atlantic link between European countries in NATO and the two North American states; the members of the HQ did not just talk about the link, they personified it.

After 9/11, the concept of transformation seized American military thinking. Many efforts inside the defence establishment became rooted in a desire to change traditional military forces into lighter, more deployable, more lethal forces. The primary proponent of this new version of military forces was Donald Rumsfeld, the US secretary of defense. Rumsfeld pushed his vision to the point where he threatened to disconnect the US from NATO if the other members did not consider this makeover. For many years, the commander of SACLANT wore two hats: he was also the commander of the US Joint Forces Command, co-located in Norfolk. Rumsfeld feared that the evolution of war-fighting strategies and the level of innovation in the US military were so rapid that other NATO nations might fall behind.

In addition, the original role of NATO as a defensive alliance of largely European nations prepared to fight on their own soil against the Soviet hordes was no longer relevant. As of 9/11, we were engaged in the war on terror. NATO nations needed to transform their forces from static ones prepared only to fight on their own territory to deployable, agile units ready to go anywhere they were needed. Rumsfeld, therefore, pushed for the establishment, in place of SACLANT, of a non-operational command focused on transformation—its area of operations would be the future. To show he was serious and to pressure other NATO nations, he withdrew the American commander from SACLANT in early 2003 and the command was handed to the deputy, Admiral Sir Ian Forbes of the UK's Royal Navy.

His tactic worked. NATO made the decision to disband SACLANT, transfer all operational responsibilities to SACEUR, and reshape it into a permanent organization solely designed to explore, develop, and implement military transformation. It was an innovative idea that was an evolution of the business innovations of the 1990s such as "change management," "continuous improvement," and "kaizen."

Two requirements underpinned transformation within NATO: one, the need for individual military forces to work together as a coherent joint force and, two, the imperative for these forces to be expeditionary. This could be as obvious as continuing to standardize weaponry among the forces deploying together to something far more complex as developing and agreeing on tactical and strategic missions and goals at the highest level. These two factors required the alliance to seek new capabilities to improve, enhance, and broaden the connectivity, deployability, flexibility, and utility of assets between member nations. What this also meant was that change was now seen as positive, something to be promoted rather than resisted.

As the last chief of staff of SACLANT, I was responsible for paving the way to make the above changes possible. Here was a place where Canada made a difference and wielded power and influence. Since the US had left the command, I was the de facto deputy on arrival and had the freedom to make decisions. My service in SACT became my last official post in uniform, and I was honoured to be recognized for that service with the NATO Meritorious Medal, the US Legion of Merit in the rank of officer, and a promotion in the Order of Military Merit to Commander.

Many other Canadians contributed to Canada's influence in NATO. The first Canadian to command the International Security and Assistance

Force (ISAF) in Afghanistan was my friend Lieutenant-General Rick Hillier, who subsequently became Canada's chief of defence. Canada's contingent grew to 2,300, the largest in ISAF, and our influence was huge because of it, especially after we undertook to look after the birthplace of the Taliban in Afghanistan, Kandahar.

Today, even though we are a founding member of NATO, Canada's financial contributions are well below the 2 percent of GDP floor required of its members. Nations including Canada committed to spending 2 percent of their GDP to defence in 2014 and reiterated the commitment as a minimum in 2023. Although the Harper government pledged to meet the target after the Crimea annexation by Russia in 2014, it never happened, and today's government has no plans to achieve it. Although only a "pledge," to me this seems a breach of contract, or at least a huge failure to live up to our commitments. The defence policy update unveiled in April 2024 provided a plan to achieve an increase to 1.76 percent but only by 2029 and no plan to get to 2 percent and beyond. Two weeks after releasing the update, the minister of National Defence stated he could not convince the cabinet of the importance of reaching that target, a sad situation indeed. You will hear the arguments that the percentage of GDP should not be the only way to measure our commitment to NATO, that Canada's defence budget is the sixth largest of all NATO nations, and that we support NATO operations fully. However, the truth is that 2 percent matters and we are woefully lacking in our commitment. This, too, contributes to the decline of our influence and our growing isolation.

Why should we remain part of NATO if we are not going to contribute adequately? The world has become more, not less, dangerous since 1949. We have threats from non-state actors, terrorism, corruption, a new "Axis of Evil," as well as state-on-state aggression and shooting wars, cyber-attacks, and everything in between. Canada is truly defenceless against many of those threats because of our government's disregard for security issues. Beyond financial contributions, our military is often unable to participate in NATO training exercises, such as Air Defender 23, its largest-ever air defence exercise. Having personally worked hard at NATO's SACT to establish interoperability between nations, and being fully committed to the idea that member nations must work together effectively and efficiently, I find our inability to participate in these exercises particularly frustrating.

From my perspective as a senior military officer, the advantage of NATO is that it is a military-political alliance; at the same time, its disadvantage is that it is a political-military alliance. Anyone who has worked with NATO can attest to the difficult, bureaucratic, and ponderous nature of its decision-making processes, certainly at the political level. The requirement for consensus means all nations must agree to a decision before it is put into effect. Recent events in Ukraine have shown us the power of an individual nation's veto (Türkiye and Hungary) and the detrimental effect it can have on progress. NATO has a process called "silence procedure" to enhance its decision-making. A potential decision (say to deploy forces to a zone of conflict) is drafted by the international staff and sent to nations' representatives in Brussels with a deadline for the silence procedure to end. In effect, if no nation raises an issue or a comment, the decision is accepted. In essence, silence is consent. Not everyone needs to say "yes," the saying goes, but no one can say "no."

Canada derives many advantages from belonging to NATO. As an institutional forum for the discussion of important global security issues, Canada stays in the know about world affairs and can attempt to influence decisions. Its constituent permanent operational headquarters are immediately able to respond to emergencies; they keep current with exercises that ensure joint multinational capability and reinforce their capability to command forces. A NATO defence innovation regional office is planned for Halifax as is a NATO Centre of Excellence on Climate Change and Security in Montréal. The whole NATO program of standardization has been a huge success and even non-NATO nations realize that they need to adopt these standards to ensure they can work with others.

I believe Canada should remain in NATO and increase its contributions, perhaps not immediately, but we should at least have a plan of incremental annual increases to reach the 2 percent threshold. There are ways to do so at the same time we increase the capabilities of the CAF.

Canada has lost the place it held for generations on the world stage and needs to recapture the hard-won influence enjoyed by our past leaders. To regain the confidence of other nations, we must first recommit ourselves to building a nation where democracy, common sense, and forthrightness prevail. A principled stand on issues must replace our current government's addiction to virtue signalling, and financial contributions must follow directly behind our stated principles. Our participation in alliances must be strengthened through our contributions, as well as voluntary participation in operations and leadership. We need to focus on the right things and then put our money where our mouth is.

CHAPTER 4

Radical Agendas

FREE-SPEECH RIGHTS ARE being trampled on in post-national Canada. The progressive government in Ottawa has tossed aside traditional Canadian values such as freedom, free speech, and tolerance to seize on a radical agenda of climate alarmism, DEI (diversity, equity and inclusion), post-nationalism and de-colonization. This has destabilized us as a nation and dampened our sense of togetherness. Proponents of the new agenda are single-minded and uncompromising. They have ordinary Canadians and leaders in the mainstream media, corporate Canada, and the national security establishment running scared. They are a blight on our civic life, and the turmoil they have caused has lowered us in the esteem of the world.

A woke mob—there's nothing else to call it—was quick to pounce on my Vimy award speech. It consisted of some of the most intolerant people in society. They weren't interested in discussing the merits of my speech or arguing another point of view. There was no opportunity for dialogue. I was given no chance to respond to their often-bizarre characterizations of my statements. They were simply out to cancel me, professionally in some instances and personally in others.

Social media is a brilliant weapon in the arsenal of the woke. No need to be brave, to have any moral fibre—just get behind that keyboard and destroy, anonymously or in the company of your like-minded followers. The mob can be frightening; it not only attacks your thoughts and ideas, it threatens you and your family with personal insults, even physical harm, and promises of more to come. When did the so-called progressives become so extreme and intolerant of other ideas and opinions?

I believe the media and their biased support of the woke agenda are much to blame. The profession has become myopic, obsessed with the left-wing values and vested in supporting leftist causes—and only leftist causes.

Although there has been much written on the media's failure to provide unbiased reporting, I think the failure became blindingly obvious during the US election of 2016. At no time in my memory has election reporting been so one-sided and the overt distaste for one candidate so applauded. The hype for Hillary Clinton's campaign was over-the-top and so appealing to the left wing that any thought of Donald Trump actually winning the election was incomprehensible. The hate for Trump became mainstream and the media not only stopped reporting fairly on the activities and views of both candidates, they began to intentionally misrepresent Trump. Edited clips of his remarks to show his comments out of context became commonplace. Clinton made many mistakes of her own, including out and out lying about certain of her past indiscretions—her failure to act on verified intelligence causing the debacle of Benghazi, her infamous destruction of 500 incriminating e-mails, and simply lying about a state visit to the former Yugoslavia that she described as harrowing when it was nothing of the sort. All of these facts were either ignored or glossed over by the media. It became so outrageous that Trump coined the phrase "fake news" and refused to speak to any legacy media.

I am not an unmitigated Trump supporter and I do not absolve him of his faults, but I had always admired the US for its respect of the democratic principles it was built upon. All this ended when Trump ran for president. After Trump won, the media afforded the sitting president zero respect and zero appreciation for the many good policies he implemented. Instead, they spent every moment since November 2016 desperately seeking to destroy him and his supporters. The cost of this battle has been extraordinary: $11.5 million on the 2019 impeachment process, $12.3 million on the Russian collusion investigation, $9 million on the classified documents scandal, $519 million and counting on the January 6 events, and more on the other prosecutions that are still ongoing at time of writing this book. And yet, he lives to run again. While the media gleefully pounces on every new charge, rumour, or investigation against Trump, Hillary Clinton's e-mails, Hunter Biden's disastrous Ukraine situation and his infamous laptop, and Joe Biden's own issues with classified documents are given a pass. The public is being fed an almost decade-long diet of partisan reporting, and the media continue to get away with it. How disrespectful to viewers and readers that we are not given the facts to decide on our own but are told how to think via a diet of left-leaning reporting.

Canada has fared little better. There was a time when op-eds were written only by seasoned journalists or experts in the field on which they were writing. This is no longer the case. As I said in November 2022, any reporter fresh out of journalism school seems allowed, perhaps even encouraged to skew the data and offer sensational takes on whatever issue they are reporting on. In my experience, few publications are prepared to air stories factually, giving equal treatment to all sides of an issue. The speech I delivered in November 2022 caused a stir but was only reported in the *National Post* and its fellow Postmedia publications. Today, there are few publications and journalists who have faith in the tenets of unbiased reporting and have not sworn allegiance to progressivism, but these are rarely mainstream and are very often labelled far-right extremists.

The journalistic malfeasance of the Trump era was given a boost in his last year in office, when the COVID pandemic hit. Headlines seemed designed to terrify the public and statistics were massaged to support preconceived narratives. "Hospitalizations increase 250 percent over long weekend," shouted one headline in the *Hamilton Spectator*, only to find, if you dug deep enough, that hospitalizations went from two people to seven.

The misinformation published during the pandemic was significant and, in some ways, understandable. We were after all dealing with a frightening unknown accompanied by many theories and guesses. But what I have a serious problem with was the systemic abandonment of a story if it proved not to be a sensation or didn't hew to a progressive narrative. There was no obligation to provide context, a correction, or an analysis of what really happened.

***

Partisanship can be found in almost all facets of our news, especially when it comes to covering our federal government. The Liberal Party has morphed from the traditional centre-left party into an intolerant, extremist, hard-left, post-national, fake-feminist movement intent on destroying our history, our values, and our democracy. Today's media absolved the prime minister of his many ethics scandals, his cultural appropriation (remember the brown-face Aladdin and the banana-in-his-underpants savage in blackface?). The "people experience things differently" groping scandal in the shade of #MeToo was tolerated and minimized in the media. Imagine the media coverage if any other Canadian politician was caught behaving this way. It certainly presents a problem when there are almost no mainstream news outlets in the country willing to publish an alternate viewpoint.

In May 2021, the media jumped on a story that 215 unmarked graves of missing children were discovered at a location in British Columbia, once the site of an Indigenous residential school (IRS). The maelstrom of self-flagellation and apologies was immediate. The story was picked up across the globe and soon bore no resemblance to the facts: "Ground penetrating radar discovery could be human remains" morphed to "Unmarked graves containing the remains of 215 Indigenous children have been discovered on the grounds of a former residential school in British Columbia." Ottawa went into overdrive and soon our flags were flying at half-mast and "genocide" became a common refrain. The flags remained at half-mast for five months and the number of children's remains purportedly buried at various IRS sites grew to 2,300. The House of Commons passed a unanimous motion in October 2022 calling for the federal government to label Canada's IRS System a genocide. Yet at the time of this writing, almost three years later, not a single body has been found or recovered. It is an astonishing indicator of how deeply this element of radical progressivism—guilt over colonization—has penetrated Canadian society.

Looking online for follow-up stories about the children's alleged graves in the media is fruitless. There are none. When the simple and logical question of whether graves have been found was raised by a columnist of the *National Post*, an op-ed headline in the *Toronto Star* blazed, "Genocide deniers ask: Where are the bodies of the residential schoolchildren? This call for the bodies of residential schoolchildren is nothing more than a racist rant bordering on genocide denial." In May 2024, Brian Griesbrecht reported in the *National Post* that $8M of taxpayers' money had been provided to Kamloops for a follow-up excavation, but nothing has been done and no one can account for the money. It seems unfathomable that there has been no move to determine whether the remains of children are there. It is even more inexplicable that families who have wondered for decades what happened to their children are given an opportunity to find out, yet they decline.

Canadians seem to have become so complacent that they willingly digest this constant diet of progressivism. But do they care about any of it? Do they care that our leaders have called us a post-nationalist state? I'm not sure they do, but I am sure they *should* care. Canadians are not outraged very often. But I find it hard to understand that Canadians would not feel slighted by our current standing in the world or the ongoing attacks on our history, culture, and mores.

A left-leaning bias is not exclusive to the media. The progressive elements of society, fed and educated by DEI-mandated ideals, are everywhere. Some have been shrouded or out of public view, but that all ended in the aftermath of Israel's 7/10 tragedy. On that fateful day, Hamas' barbaric murderers broke through the border fences and walls and committed unspeakable acts against innocent Israeli and foreign citizens. Since then, we have seen the result of the anti-colonial, anti-white mindset on free speech on our streets and in our universities. There is only one voice allowed and it is filled with hate.

***

Universities have long been the site of passionate debates—young minds learning about the world and learning how to think are brimming with passion. But the days of passionate and healthy debate are long over on our campuses. The days of protesters marching on both sides of an issue are relegated to history.

My wife speaks fondly of a history professor she studied under years ago who encouraged his students to debate, but with a twist. He would send them back in time to debate issues that history has long judged appalling but to find arguments, context, logic, reasoning, whether justified or not, for the behaviour of our fellow men in those days. By researching both sides of an issue, by forcing his students to debate for the "guilty" side, his pupils were often able to understand the historical significance of an event more fully. The Civil War was debated by both the abolitionists and the slave owners, and also by the cotton merchants, tobacco sellers, expansionists, and those in favour of the right of states to invalidate federal legislation. The debates were lively and friendly, with history providing the outcome. But much was learned about the difficulty of governing a huge country such as the United States which, like Canada, encompasses a vast territory, numerous industries, natural resources, and a diverse population. In history classes focusing on the causes of WW2, students found themselves examining the emergence of the German National Socialist Party and absorbing the lessons learned from the exorbitant reparations placed on Germany and its citizens post

WW1 that gave Hitler a pretext for grievance and fuelled his rise to power and creation of the Third Reich. The point wasn't to engender sympathy for Nazism but to open students' eyes to how tragedies occur. Understanding not just what happened but why it happened should help future leaders recognize the danger signs and ensure the world never creates such a situation again.

None of that nuance is allowed today. There is only *one* point of view, *one* narrative to be taught. Students these days are taught *what* to think, not *how* to think. And they have become vicious and intolerant in their righteousness—so much so that anyone with questions, never mind an opposing viewpoint, is terrified of speaking out. And all these attitudes are based on the tenets of a radical progressive agenda: DEI, colonialism, the equation of merit with white supremacy, climate alarmism, and so on.

The attack by Hamas terrorists on Israel on October 7 had blatant genocidal intent. The live-streamed glee of the Hamas murderers should have shaken every person on earth; Hamas leaders' vow that "Operation Al-Aqsa Flood" was just an opening act and would happen "again and again and again" should have set the stage for universal outrage and a commitment to the complete destruction of Hamas. Instead, we've adopted a simple-minded narrative in which Israelis, portrayed as white and Jewish, are deplored as colonizers and Palestinians are positioned as the colonized. Everything is reduced to the critical-race-theory binary of oppressor vs oppressed.

It appears our federal government has bought into such blather. These were despicable acts of violence—the worst committed against Jews since the Holocaust. They were the sort of thing that should make anyone sick, and they were extensively (and proudly) documented by the perpetrators, yet it took two months and tremendous pressure for our foreign affairs minister to condemn these acts.

Our embassy in Tel Aviv was no better, saying, "we must acknowledge that Israeli women and girls have been profoundly impacted by the ongoing conflict between Israel and Hamas. Accounts of brutal sexual violence during the October 7 Hamas attacks are deeply concerning and must be investigated." Investigated? There is gruesome footage and firsthand accounts of this brutality and the very best our feminist PM and his government can muster is this? Academia was even worse. Samantha Pearson, director of the University of Alberta's Sexual Assault Centre, signed an open letter denying women were raped at all. What happened to "believe all women"? Within the tenets of radical progressive ideology, crimes perpetrated by a so-called oppressed minority upon so-called white colonists don't count. Yes, Pearson was eventually fired by the university, but it must be acknowledged that much damage had been done and that her outlook is still a common one among the professoriate.

* * *

The protests following October 7 have continued unabated under the protection of the right to free speech. Radical progressives seem to be the only group left for whom these rights still exist. All over the world, people gather in the hundreds and thousands waving Palestinian flags, draped in keffiyehs, praising the murders as acts of resistance, an understandable effort to rid "their homeland" of the Jewish occupiers. Young women with bare midriffs and LGBTQ2+ supporters under "Queers for Palestine" rainbow banners marched, shouting, "From the river to the sea, Palestine will be free!" They were oblivious, or ignorant, to the fact that their own existence and appearance in Gaza would come with significant consequences, including fines, arrest, and worse.

If there is any question about the selective enforcement of free speech rights in Canada, think back to when the Freedom Convoy rolled into Ottawa in January 2022. Protesting COVID restrictions and vaccine mandates, these truckers and their supporters were demanding an audience with the prime minister, something they requested weeks before they arrived in Ottawa. Justin Trudeau refused to meet with them; instead, he dismissed them as a "small fringe minority" with "unacceptable views."

He later accused them of championing "hate, abuse and racism." The protest was eventually dismantled by the invocation of the Emergencies Measures Act, which included freezing the bank accounts of convoy supporters and mandating tow trucks to remove the trucks parked in Ottawa. Invocation of that act was ruled unconstitutional early in 2024, but the country remains divided.

There is no doubt the right of free speech was not afforded to the convoy participants. When the statue of Terry Fox in downtown Ottawa was draped in a Canadian flag, the protesters were eviscerated by the media, the government, and many Canadians for an act tantamount to vandalism. When the same statue was draped in a Palestinian keffiyeh during an anti-Israel protest, it was met with silence from the same cohort. I am certain there were many Canadians offended and sickened by this desecration, but they were too afraid to speak out. Our legacy media, of course, were silent.

* * *

The government's emphasis on Diversity, Equity, and Inclusion, and especially its unique brand of "feminism," has disgracefully overtaken meritocracy. The need to appoint women to positions, qualified or not, is mind-boggling. Our most recent governors-general, Mary Simon and Julie Payette, are glaring examples of virtue signalling gone bad. Were they really the best representatives of our country and was there any vetting? Simon is a lifelong diplomat who became governor-general without being able to speak French, one of Canada's two official languages. Two and a half years later, no discernable linguistic progress has been made. A group of Quebecers called for her appointment to be rescinded in 2021, and the case remains to be heard by the Quebec Superior Court. I find it inconceivable that a Canadian career diplomat who rose to the level of ambassador never desired, nor was required, to learn French. I find it hypocritical that she could build her entire career on fighting for the rights of one Canadian minority, the Inuit, while completely ignoring another, French-speaking Canadians. Members of our Canadian Armed Forces are often drawn from our immigrant communities, and they are masters of a variety of languages. But make no mistake: their ascension in rank is limited without proficiency in both of Canada's official languages. I know this is so across the public service and all government departments at the national level.

Julie Payette's lack of leadership and a charge of second-degree assault in Maryland (later dismissed) should have raised a red flag during any process to vet her for an appointment as governor-general. Payette proved to be a toxic boss, to the extent that an independent inquiry was launched, its findings leading to her resignation in early 2021. That was the second time she resigned a post due to her behaviour. The inquiry found that she had "belittled, berated and publicly humiliated Rideau Hall staff" and "created a toxic, verbally abusive workplace."

The prime minister takes no responsibility for these mistakes in judgment and Canadians do not respond. These women ticked the boxes of his fixation on DEI and fake feminism and, therefore, were appointed to positions for which they were unsuited. Though the prime minister calls himself a twenty-first-century feminist, we have had many reasons to doubt his true commitment to the advancement of women. Two of the most qualified women in his original cabinet, Jody Wilson-Raybould and Jane Philpott, were expelled from or left his caucus as a result of the SNC-Lavalin affair, yet another example of Trudeau's inexplicable inability to understand the simplest definition of ethical behaviour. Although his interference in Wilson-Raybould's prosecution of SNC-Lavalin was undeniable, even recorded, Trudeau escaped unscathed. She was given the boot, unbelievably, for not showing "confidence in the Liberal government" as indicated by her decision to record her conversation with the clerk of the Privy Council. Philpott, who was a loyal supporter of Wilson-Raybould, resigned to signify that support and was also expelled from caucus.

* * *

The #MeToo movement against sexual abuse, sexual harassment, and rape culture especially in the workplace has changed the landscape of all our interactions. Hopefully, it has rid many organizations of predators and made everyone aware of the despicable behaviours that caused so much damage to women. In many cases, long-overdue justice was rained down upon perpetrators like Harvey Weinstein. But like many movements, #MeToo also has a downside.

In the initial stages of revelations of sexual harassment in the workplace, the notion of always believing the women caused its own share of damage. In some instances, we seemed to remove the burden-of-proof requirement, and even the need for due process. Many men's lives were ruined, unfairly, by unproven accusations. Once again, the media (particularly social media) played no small role in these miscarriages of justice. Quick to pounce on the accusations and publicly label the accused, the story was quickly dropped or relegated to a brief note if the evidence failed to support the charges. In our zeal to bring perpetrators to justice and shed light on this sinister phenomenon, we neglected to follow through. What happens if the case has no merit? What if a woman is not telling the truth? We had, and still have, little recourse for victims if they are men who are falsely accused. In the military, this miscarriage of justice proved fatal for several honourable soldiers who were removed from their posts, forbidden to wear the uniforms they earned, and when found not guilty of the crimes they were accused of, not allowed back on duty.

Beyond its inherent unfairness, what message does it send to the young women in an organization who are capable of so much more than being told to treat every interaction with a man as a possible misconduct? I'm not sure this has fostered the teamwork necessary for success in any organization.

One would imagine the prime minister, as a self-proclaimed feminist, to be unshakable in standing with women. No. Although settled out of court accompanied by a non-disclosure agreement, details emerged of an incident between Trudeau and a young reporter that took place at a fundraising event in British Columbia years ago. The CBC reported in July 2018 that "an unsigned editorial appeared in the *Creston Valley Advance* after the event accusing the prime minister of 'groping' and 'inappropriately handling' a young female reporter while she was on assignment." It suggests the woman felt "blatantly disrespected," but provides no other details about what occurred. When questioned about the incident, the prime minister responded, "The same interactions can be experienced very differently from one person to the next" and "I am confident that I did not act inappropriately," and, finally, "I am not going to speak for the woman in question. I would never presume to speak for her. But I know that there is an awful lot of reflection to be had as we move forward as a society on how people perceive different interactions."

In other words, he did nothing wrong, she obviously was mistaken, and this is a teaching moment for "society," not for him. In this particular case, the woman was *not* believed and her feelings of discomfort at being groped and blatantly disrespected were passed off as figments of her imagination. Undoubtedly, in retrospect, she ought to change her story. Imagine for a moment if these allegations had emerged about the leader of the opposition or anyone, for that matter, who does not toe the Liberal party line. The outrage by the prime minister would have been incredible.

But where is the outrage from Canadians?

***

Going forward, radical progressivism must be abandoned. Canadians must shed their complacency and demand a return to the values and principles that defined us in the past—equality, the rule of law, fairness, national security—and need to define us in the future. The prevarication must stop. If it doesn't, Canada will be unable to take a stance on issues that require judgment to be based on standards of law and good order.

A nation that is afraid to condemn blatant acts of terrorism and racism because they may offend those of the DEI minorities is not acting on behalf of its citizens.

Free speech must become a reality for all sides of every issue. Hate speech must be punished. The mainstream media must be forced back to responsible journalism; Canadians deserve the truth and the facts—all the facts—and be allowed to form their own conclusions. We must insist that the media uphold the principles of professional and ethical journalism.

Universities must return to the lofty heights of learning, of teaching their students how to think for themselves—how to embrace facts and critically analyze them to arrive at sound and just conclusions. The DEI narrative must be removed and replaced with equal opportunity and inclusive meritocracy for all. That is the very definition of reaching the height of success through hard work and fair competition.

Governments, those of today and of the future, must go back to governing for the good of the people, not for the pleasure of one special-interest group at the cost of others. These changes will help Canada retake its place on the world stage, restoring its image as a fair and kind democratic society willing and able to protect human rights at home and abroad.

CHAPTER 5

DEI, Democracy, and Meritocracy

DIVERSITY, EQUITY, AND INCLUSION is a successor to affirmative action, first put into practice in the US by an executive order issued by President Kennedy in 1961. The order included a provision that government contractors "take affirmative action to ensure that applicants are employed, and employees are treated [fairly] during employment, without regard to their race, creed, colour, or national origin." This was a good idea and necessary at the time of the burgeoning American civil rights movement aimed at righting the wrongs perpetrated on black Americans since the end of slavery. DEI is different. It is a rampant and dangerous ideology having negative effects on every facet of society.

For most of its existence, affirmative action kept true to the tenet that it was not designed to replace merit or induce hiring quotas, but that has changed in the DEI era. The extremes to which DEI has taken over the public consciousness have rendered meritocracy obsolete and incited a new form of discrimination. Quotas loom large in hiring practices and some institutions (notably universities) place DEI principles over all other qualifications in job applicants. That these hiring practices have led to a decline in qualitative output has become obvious. The emerging data is hard to ignore. At the time of writing, there appears to be the beginnings of a backlash brewing and time will tell if common sense prevails.

A perfect example of DEI going awry was the hiring of Claudine Gay as president of Harvard University. She ticked many intersectional boxes, including being black and female, but she was woefully underqualified for the job. She was academically undistinguished, having published just eleven academic articles in her career. Her lack of academic credentials didn't matter because the DEI narrative was more important than the historical qualifications of academic integrity and experience in her field. She eventually resigned in the wake of numerous plagiarism charges, but will be forever remembered for her astonishing inability during a US congressional hearing in December 2023 to answer yes to the question, "Does calling for the genocide of Jews violate Harvard's rules on bullying and harassment?"

DEI has evolved from its affirmative action-based intent, which aimed to ensure the same opportunities are available to all persons regardless of race, sexual orientation, gender identity, or religion, and to welcome and treat all persons with respect. DEI has instead become a form of discrimination against any person who cannot be identified as a victim of colonization, marginalization, or oppression. Gay and the other two university presidents who appeared in that December congressional hearing proved to be so focused on the colonizer-vs-colonized theme that they could not bring themselves to admit that the hateful and threatening protests taking place on their campuses created an unsafe space and racist environment for their Jewish students.

The insidious DEI principle has filled our public service and academic institutions with people whose only goal is to promote this agenda. Ticking the boxes of DEI is the only prerequisite for the job. Laith Marouf was given $133,000 and hired as a senior consultant on an anti-racist project sponsored by the federal government. I will not quote the outrageously vile and disgusting anti-Semitic comments made by him on his X account, but they are still floating around the Internet. After the scandal over his tweets erupted in 2022, the government said its housing, diversity and inclusion minister "would look closely at the situation" and launch a probe into the offending tweets. Canadians should be outraged by the fact that this bigot was given a job in the first place, let alone funding in an anti-racism project sponsored by our tax dollars. It's made worse by the fact that the minister responsible for this disgraceful and embarrassing situation is still serving.

A seemingly well-intentioned concept transformed into a blatant, racist, unforgiving and tunnel-visioned ideal, DEI has become ingrained among social justice zealots and other members of our self-congratulating society. Universities have begun to consider themselves places of white supremacy, racist, unsafe for anyone of colour or who belonged to the LGBTQ2+ minority. This imbalance, the progressives decried, had to be fixed by removing meritocracy from the hiring and admission processes. Minorities had to take precedence, and their inclusion, to the exclusion of all others, took priority. Was there really a problem? And how does the extreme DEI ideal fix it? How does it promote equal opportunity or unity? Those were the ultimate goals of the civil rights movement and affirmative action. Going back as far as the Reverend Martin Luther King's "I Have a Dream" speech, he emphasized the importance of everyone being treated equally, which is contrary to the goals of DEI. He famously said, "I have a dream that my four little children will one day live in a nation where they will not be judged by the colour of their skin but by the content of their character."

How would the reverend feel about his children now being judged solely on the colour of their skin with little or no concern for the content of their character? Character matters little to the DEI standard. In today's DEI-obsessed world, education, experience, and talent once again take a back seat to the colour of your skin. Today, his children would have no idea if they were given the job, promotion, or opportunity because they merited it or simply because they were black. I can't help but believe this is not progress.

When the PM introduced his cabinet in 2015, he was asked why 50 percent were women. The self-proclaimed feminist replied, "because it's 2015!" Canadian media loved it, as did Liberal partisans. But what could be more *anti-feminist* than that response? Instead of saying, "I looked at all the MPs in my caucus and I chose the best and brightest and most talented to form my cabinet, and no one should be surprised that 50 percent of them are women," he threw out a flippant sound bite that immediately planted seeds of doubt among all Canadians and undoubtedly his caucus that perhaps the best were not selected—that perhaps 50 percent got the job simply because they were women, filling a personal quota he intended to meet regardless of suitability.

If meritocracy has no place in the selection of the cabinet, what are the consequences? Imagine the women chosen and how they might question their appointment: "Did I get the job because I am the best suited, or did I get it because I am a woman?" Now imagine the men who were not chosen. Did his sound bite assure them the most qualified were chosen to lead this new government, or do they feel they were overlooked simply because they are not women? However you care to measure this exchange, I think it is fair to say that it does not foster a sense of teamwork, equality, or inclusion.

What of the gay Indigenous cabinet minister who may well be the most qualified for the position? Does he question whether he got the job on merit or simply because of his orientation and/or ethnicity? Are his co-workers satisfied that the chosen candidate was hired only on the basis of DEI? Do they shrug at his capabilities, or lack thereof, or harbour resentment because merit was not considered? It is hard to imagine the workplace not filled with animosity, confusion, and feelings of exclusion.

Today, DEI is firmly entrenched in our academic institutions, from kindergarten through graduate school. Given its near-universal presence, it is useful to ask what effect it has had. Has it transformed any of the institutions into success stories? Has it made successful ones even more so? Evidence indicates the answer is no. When any institution wants to undergo change, it needs to be rigorous in how it proceeds. When change is contemplated, it is usually because an area is failing or needs improvement. The first order of business is to identify the problem, the issue that needs improvement or the new path to be followed. In essence, what is prompting the change? This first step must be followed by a proposed course of action that will move the institution from failure to success. The process needs to embed several metrics aimed at monitoring and measuring the effectiveness of the change, accompanied by a timeline and a target.

This is not the case with the integration of DEI. Simply saying it exists in your institution seems to prove its success. There are no mechanisms to evaluate success, no timelines, not even a targeted end-state. Most importantly, there is no opportunity to ask challenging questions or to debate its effectiveness. There is only one narrative, and proposing any deviation is dangerous. Speaking as a survivor of DEI's favoured enforcement mechanism, cancel culture, I can tell you that pushing back is not pleasant. If you dare question the accepted narrative, you will quickly and vehemently be labelled a racist, bigot, misogynist, and more. Only the accepted ideals, those that are celebrated and encouraged and applauded by the DEI apostles, are allowed. Opposing viewpoints, even simple questions, are dealt with in an adversarial environment and discouraged. There is no room for respectful debate, there is no room for dialogue.

I have been unable to find measured success stories specifically tied to the implementation of the DEI ideal at the expense of the majority. There are many testimonials from businesses and organizations that, via anecdote, credit DEI with making their workplaces more welcoming and inclusive, boosting the well-being and productivity of the workforce. But statistics detailing the increased productivity in terms of output or profit remain unseen. There are firm examples, on the other hand, of forcing DEI into a business plan with disastrous results. Take a look at the recent financials for Disney or Bud Light, two brands that embraced radical progressivism and pushed it on their customer bases. Consumers know when a brand is acting with integrity and when it's merely trying to curry favour with special-interest groups. The latter appears to be a recipe for disaster.

Absurdly, DEI zealots consider the suggestion that democracy and meritocracy should still have a place in our world as racist and bigoted. Imagine a professional sports team eliminating meritocracy from its player selection and implementing the DEI approach instead. One can look at the National Football League as an example of removing barriers to opportunity, but retaining meritocracy. According to ESPN, in the 1960s, only 16.5 percent of NFL players were black. Today that number has increased to 58 percent and that ratio is even higher in the National Basketball Association. Imagine imposed DEI precepts forcing these teams to accept more white or Indigenous or Hispanic players simply on the basis of their race.

There are many ordinary Canadians who want to debate the merits of DEI policies but are afraid to speak out. But being attacked on social media or by work colleagues can be frightening, so they remain silent while the frustration simmers. It may one day bubble over. It may already be doing so: it appears the backlash has begun and the tide is starting to turn. Make no mistake, loosening DEI's hold on our institutions cannot happen overnight as it has become deeply integrated into our world. It may take generations to walk back the damage caused.

Interestingly, the backlash may well be happening in academia, the very wellspring of DEI whose institutions have created a cohort of true believers that, upon graduation, are either released into society or occupy positions in all levels of our education system, top to bottom. In the opening months of 2024, alumni of Harvard and the University of Pennsylvania (both of whose presidents resigned following the US congressional testimony disaster) have put millions of dollars in donations to their alma maters in question, which may have a significant impact. There are some who have tried to say that President Gay was forced to resign from Harvard because she is black. Luckily, that argument seems to have gained no traction. In Canada, I know of at least one university (McMaster in Hamilton, Ont.) that is facing withdrawal of financial support over its stance on anti-Semitism connected with the aftermath of the October 7 massacre of Israelis. One way or another, I believe the concept of meritocracy, which in its purest form is the fairest of criteria and provides the greatest chance of success for all people, will make a comeback.

It is time to be realistic. If our society is to succeed, our obsession with social justice needs to be touched with the wand of reality. There is no need to abandon the dreams such heroes as Martin Luther King Jr or John F. Kennedy had for equal opportunity based on merit and talent, not on skin colour or pronouns or religion. Theirs was a virtuous ambition. Implementing what one can call inclusive meritocracy—a notion I first heard from my friend Dr John Scott Cowan, that *only* when two candidates are equal can immutable identities like race, ethnicity, disability or gender influence a hiring or promotion decision—is a good place to start. But even with this much preferred system, there must be a defined end-state: what is our goal? If it's an even-playing field, how will we know when we're there? A tough question indeed and not one any institution or government is willing to consider at this time. Fairness in a democracy is a messy business. The path to solutions won't be quick or easy.

* * *

Democracy is defined most simply as "rule by the people." A nation is considered a democracy if those who govern are given their power by the people via fair and free elections. Democracy, though a relatively new human invention on a civilizational time scale, has been an ideal of people everywhere. Countless wars have been fought, and monarchies and totalitarian states have been overthrown through revolutions and coups, to achieve democracy. The creation of the United States, the greatest power in the world, was based on such a revolution. Freedom is

DEI, DEMOCRACY, AND MERITOCRACY

considered an essential tenet of democracy, and history has shown that most democratic countries inherently protect human rights, freedom of expression, economic development, and the rule of law. Democracy was once the ultimate ideal for all the world.

Like meritocracy, however, democracy has faced serious headwinds of late and sadly, the "silent majority" has stayed silent. Forcing the DEI agenda on the world has eroded the freedom and rights inherent in democracies; the majority no longer rules. The obsession to give minorities and special-interest groups a voice—also an essential part of democracy— has mutated into an assault on the majority. It is most obviously manifest in the silencing and sidelining of that majority, which is extremism at its worst. Inclusivity has lost its definition. In the simplest of terms, why does one voice have to be erased to allow another? The very definition of inclusive is to embrace *all* voices, ideals, religions, and colour; sadly, that is not the case today. Anything that doesn't conform to the DEI agenda is offensive and must be erased. It can take many seemingly trivial forms: erasing a historical figure who doesn't fit the mould, removing a Christmas tree in front of city hall, censoring a library book that uses the language of the time in which it was written. Offensive, triggering, microaggressions—these terms have come to define the culture of what is still a majority of Canadians.

Democracy runs the gamut of experience, from a national election with global consequences to a hockey team choosing pizza or burgers after the game. In a democracy, if ten of the twelve hockey players want pizza, pizza it is. The other two either eat pizza or find something else to eat on their own. Not anymore. In today's world, if one person is "offended" by the Christmas tree at city hall, down it comes, despite 87 percent of Canadians surveyed saying they celebrate Christmas. How is this acceptable in a country that proclaims itself a democracy? I have no problem with inclusion, and I believe most Canadians don't. If I see a menorah, or am wished "Happy Kwanzaa," I'm not offended. In fact, I welcome the opportunity to learn more about holidays celebrated by other ethnicities and religions. What a wonderful world it would be if everyone, rather than be offended, welcomed differences and joined in the celebrations. Isn't that true inclusivity? Democracy has been replaced with obsessive attention to the special-interest groups and minorities across the country to the exclusion of the majority.

These culture clashes have sadly found a home in the Canadian Armed Forces, a situation that causes me much grief. As a thirty-five-year veteran, I can say that I was proud to don that uniform every day of my career. On international missions and travelling across the globe, the red maple leaf on my shoulder garnered respect and admiration. As I have discussed, it is no secret that I no longer feel our men and women in uniform have the same place on the world stage. The CAF has placed DEI above operational readiness and capability. While our soldiers are forced to visit food banks and buy their own helmets, Ottawa continues its obsession with culture change.

I have it said it before but will emphasize it here: the culture of the military that allowed for racist and misogynist behaviour needed to change. I will also say that this was recognized before the events of January 2021 broke in the media. We were not completely successful in eliminating the issues, but the problem was identified and steps were being taken. Since then, the pendulum has swung so far the other way that the CAF has become hardly recognizable—literally. The $144.3 million allocated to culture change over five years has produced changes, yes: to the dress regulations allowing such non-uniform items as man-buns, coloured nail polish, facial hair and tattoos, and the option of wearing skirts for men. CAF members are forced to identify their pronouns, and several ceremonial or historical traditions have been eliminated. It is an attempt to make the CAF a poster organization for DEI, while neglecting most service members who do not belong to any of the minority groups championed by the DEI narrative.

Let's see how this is working out. It is no secret the military is facing a huge personnel shortage. At the time of writing, 16,500 positions are unfilled. Making the military inclusive was intended to aid in retention of currently serving personnel and encourage recruiting of Canadians across the country. Instead, recruiting numbers in the CAF in 2022–23 were 5,242, down from the previous year's 8,069, a reduction of 34 percent. According to *Blacklock's Reporter*, regular members who quit the CAF outnumbered new recruits by as much as 19 percent over the past three years.

The statistics seem to illustrate that the culture change so championed by the military has had no effect boosting recruitment, but what no one is saying it that the change does not appeal to the majority of serving members or prospective recruits. Of all the Canadians who serve in the military, 71 percent are white males. Women make up 16 percent of members, 2.8 percent are Indigenous and 9.4 percent visible minorities. Although I was unable to find a percentage of serving members who belong to the LGBTQ2+ demographic, in Canada as a whole Statistics Canada reports that in 2022, 4 percent of the population over age 15 identifies with one or more elements of this demographic. And yet, an unfathomable number of resources, money and staff, are poured into the recruitment of these minorities with no measurable result.

Common sense would dictate that while welcoming every Canadian regardless of race, sexual orientation, religion, and ethnicity should be essential and sincere, we should be directing at least some of our recruiting efforts to the majority, attracting those Canadians most likely to serve. It stands to reason that in any democracy, the fulfilment of the majority will result in better outcomes.

* * *

Democracy is the foremost ideal on which the greatest nations of the world including ours were founded. To abandon the principles of democracy—free, fair, and inclusive electoral processes, diverse, inclusive, and pluralistic legislatures, adherence to the rule of law, and the promotion and protection of human rights—is a big step back for our nation.

Historically, meritocracy has proved to be the most successful method of hiring and promoting the best person for the job. The concept of merit is unarguably fair and inclusive. The best outcomes will be achieved with the best people at the helm. Give Canadians some credit for recognizing imbalances and making the changes necessary to foster success: use inclusive meritocracy. The success of one group of individuals does not have to come at the expense of another. Working together is the way to achieve this goal. Merit does not see colour, sexual orientation, ethnicity, or religion; it sees only merit.

DEI has eroded these democratic principles upon which Canada was founded. Our great history proves these concepts are successful. It's time to swing the pendulum back to common sense. Democracy and meritocracy cannot continue to be sacrificed to the extremism of DEI. We can do better.

CHAPTER 6

The Climate and Our Resources

IGH ATOP THE PROGRESSIVE agenda sits climate. Fear-mongering and doomsday predictions have everyone terrified. The insistence on pursuing zero-emissions policies is wreaking havoc on our economy and crippling our extractive industries, which, like it or not, are the backbone of the Canadian economy. Gatekeepers in government are trying to strangle any initiative that doesn't meet their impossible goal of keeping fossil fuels in the ground. Carbon taxes are hurting all Canadians and causing regional discord because of their unequal implementation. In short, the panic over climate change and the false narratives it has generated are destabilizing society and threatening our way of life.

Climate change has become an obsession for our leaders. The World Economic Forum surveyed almost 1,500 leaders in 2023 and asked them what they believed to be the greatest global risks for 2024. Climate change topped the list at 66 percent. Compare this with a large survey in 2020 by AIDATA of low- and middle-income countries that placed climate twelfth out of sixteen issues (although some progressive governments of developed countries have caught the fever and begun prioritizing the climate "crisis" above even development aid).

Aided by the media, the UN and its alarmist-in-chief, Secretary-General António Guterres, have been on a crusade to scare the bejesus out of everyone about the fate of our planet if we do not reduce our carbon footprint. Schoolchildren are stressed about the future of their world and the damage our generation is doing to the earth.

Canada is caught up in these trends. Our government and the media have convinced Canadians that we are in a crisis and that Canada can quickly transition from oil and gas to alternative sources of energy, fix the climate and stop global warming. It is a preposterous idea—Canada contributes only 1.6 percent of the world's greenhouse gas emissions so eliminating these entirely would have little effect—but many Canadians have completely swallowed the hook.

Our prime minister renamed his government's Department of the Environment, calling it Environment and Climate Change Canada, and appointed as its minister an environmental extremist, Steven Guilbeault, who once worked for Greenpeace. In 2001, Guilbeault climbed the CN Tower in Toronto to protest the lack of effort to ratify the Kyoto Protocol and called Canada and US president George W Bush climate killers. Apparently exhausted and unable to climb back down, he and his companion endangered the first responders and workers who had to erect scaffolding in the pouring rain to rescue these tired souls. I have been unable to find a price tag for this foolhardy endeavour.

The Trudeau government has placed green issues above affordable housing, health care, national security—everything. Instead of a measured approach to a long-term problem, we have declared an emergency and taken the same uncompromising attitude to climate change that we've applied to so many other items on the radical progressive agenda. There is only one correct point of view. No other voices are permissible. Our government and media ignore each new study, each new proof that obsessions with electric vehicles and solar power or wind-produced energy will not work in Canada's vast and cold country. They also ignore all of the research and investment that have gone into climate mitigation strategies to reduce the carbon footprint of oil-and-gas extraction and usage in Canada.

What I also find preposterous is that in all the discussions, no one looks at the great strides we have made in so many sectors. Prime Minister Mulroney's efforts helped curb acid rain and our lakes have now recovered. The ozone hole which had opened up has been closed. Thirty years ago, radio stations would report the pollution index daily; they don't do it any more because air pollution has been greatly reduced. The Canadian energy sector has done a lot to clean up the industry. According to the Canadian Energy Centre, methane emissions targets from the sector have been achieved way ahead of schedule. Emissions from oil sands have remained flat despite growth in production; companies have spent huge amounts on cleaning up inactive wells, facilities, and pipelines, according to the Alberta Energy Regulator. Freshwater use has decreased through recycling so that our lakes, rivers, and shallow groundwater are protected. Technology and private R&D will continue to make efforts to reduce the environmental impact of oil and gas production. Our energy sector is doing its part, yet our government wants only to march arm-in-arm with Greta Thunberg and her ridiculous war on fossil fuels. What an incredible difference we could be making to the climate if only common sense prevailed.

I want to be clear that I am not a climate change denier. I am skeptical that global warming is entirely man-made, and even more skeptical that we can control the climate through public policy, but I try to keep an open mind and I think climate issues are serious enough to warrant debate. In my time as academic director of Royal Military College Saint-Jean, the climate panic had already begun and I thought it would be beneficial to hold a symposium on climate change where we would invite a group of climate scientists to a debate. We could have some who were on the side of "climate change is all man-made" and some who believed climate change was a natural phenomenon and that while man could not stop the climate from changing, he could mitigate some of the damage.

I thought this would provide faculty and students the opportunity to witness a scientific debate and open a dialogue to discuss both sides of this contentious issue. I was wrong. The very notion of exposing the students to an opinion contrary to the popular alarmist theory, of daring to question the usual narrative, was ruled out of bounds. To this day, I am sorry I did not push through with this.

Canadians need to push back against climate alarmism and a government that puts photo ops and virtue signalling at international summits ahead of our economic welfare. Ottawa is so caught up in the race to meet unrealistic emissions targets and dismantle our natural resource sector that we're missing out on our best opportunities to make a real difference when it comes to safeguarding the environment. It is entirely possible to develop common-sense policies that will allow Canada to help reduce global warming and help the environment writ large without abandoning oil-and-gas development and killing our economy.

The first objective of a common-sense environmental strategy should be for Canada to become self-sufficient in energy. We are currently importing oil from other nations, some of which are illiberal, because Ottawa refuses to approve and push through pipelines that would allow our own resources to be transported across the country. Second, we were in the past the US's largest foreign supplier of oil; we should advocate with our southern neighbours to return to this status, thereby aiding continental energy security, and bolstering the Canadian economy. Third, we can become the world's leading supplier of cleaner energy to foster a change from coal-fired energy production while allowing time for nations to transition. Fourth, Canadian industry, with support from the government, should be encouraged to continue development of reliable and safe nuclear energy, including small modular reactors, the first of which is set to open in Ontario. Our aging Candu system is already recognized globally for its quality and reliability.

Canada is blessed with huge natural resources—fresh water, fossil fuels, rare minerals, agricultural land, and almost infinite forests that capture more carbon than Canada emits. Instead of dismissing our allies' pleas for natural gas because there is no real business case to do so (the current PM's contention, which has proved to be nonsense), we could become leaders in helping the world transition to a greener energy future. The US cut CO_2 output by 20 percent over the last two decades by using more natural gas and less coal. We could help other countries do the same, but that would require us to support our energy industry, not drive it into the ground.

Natural disasters have a huge impact on emissions. Citing data from government and other sources, the Insurance Bureau of Canada found that we succeeded in reducing our annual national industrial emissions by 62 megatonnes between 2005 and 2021, arriving at 670 megatonnes. But in the summer of 2023 alone, a group of 5,000 wildfires were responsible for emitting an estimated 480 megatonnes.

Many have said this before: Canada is a small polluter compared to China, India, Brazil, or the US. We produce only 1.6 percent of the world's carbon emissions. Driving Canada back to the stone age would make very little difference to global warming. But our much-maligned resource sector could be used to help other countries transition to greener energy, and that could have a very significant impact on the world's emissions.

David Knight Legg, former advisor to the premier of Alberta and chairman of Elements Advisors, an investment firm in Asia, states that "according to IHS Markit, Canada's gas has the quality, proximity, and cost advantages that make it a natural contender to decarbonize the grid in China and across India. Trading into just 20 percent of the Asian grid would remove more emissions from the planet than Canada's entire carbon footprint."

A Fraser Institute post in November 2021 made a similar comment: "If the Trudeau government had not cancelled the Northern Gateway pipeline, which was designed to facilitate exports to Asia, Canada would be in a much stronger position to offer a realistic win-win alternative for oil and gas production and emissions. Canada could increase production and export larger volumes to China, reducing that country's need for greater coal power. That means a reduction in global Green House Gasses (GHG) because coal, which has higher GHG emissions, would be replaced by natural gas and/or oil, which has lower GHG emissions."

Exporting more of our abundant and relatively clean-burning natural gas would not only help the developing world phase out much of its coal, it would be a tremendous win for Canada's stagnant economy. Like it or not, natural resources, and oil and gas in particular, will be our national advantage for the foreseeable future. Statistics Canada in 2023 valued Canada's energy assets at more than seventy-five times the country's other natural resources combined. Our oil, gas, and coal assets alone were worth $1.6 trillion in 2022 compared to $907 billion for forest timber and minerals. At the same time, the International Energy Agency reported that the world demand for oil and gas continues to rise and is now at about 100 million barrels of oil per day. We have a lot of what the world needs.

I find it incredible to believe that our natural gas cannot be better developed and used to help other nations wean themselves off their coal addiction. Many have called on the Canadian government to accelerate the building of an energy economy that would prioritize liquefied natural gas (LNG), with export terminals on our east and west coasts. Instead, the prime minister states without evidence that there is no business case for the export of LNG. Eventually, the world might reduce the need for oil and LNG-based energy and transition to renewables and nuclear, but that is not an overnight solution. For the next fifty years at least, Canada could help the world with this intermediate step.

The attitude of the federal government has completely tied the hands of private developers. Take Ottawa's anti-pipeline stance, for instance. In March 2023, Spanish energy giant Repsol abandoned plans for developing an LNG plant in New Brunswick in order to supply Germany and other European nations hindered by the lack of Russian gas. It would have faced a huge hurdle trying to secure enough gas from western Canada and then ship it internally without a pipeline. These types of decisions by Canadian

THE CLIMATE AND OUR RESOURCES

gatekeepers not only waste Canadian resources, but do not help the rest of the world accomplish its green goals, and all of those global emissions targets that Canada likes to sign on to are missed again and again.

In addition to making our natural gas available to the world, Canada's environmental policy should focus on the protection of our water resources, reduction in plastic use, recycling of paper products, management of our forests, greening of our agricultural sector, and the greenest extraction and use of fossil fuels possible. In terms of mitigation of climate change, since it is inevitable, we should think of what we can do to prepare. For example, if sea levels rise, how can we protect or move populations living in low-lying areas? If wildfires continue to occur at greater rates in more areas, how can we improve our forest management and firefighting capabilities? At the time of writing, it looks like we are in for another summer of wildfires. Firefighting assets should be of the highest quality and efficiency. Forestry companies should be encouraged to take part in forest management including clearing dangerous underbrush at the same time as they harvest this great resource. At-risk populations living in wooded areas should be encouraged to have emergency plans. The remaining above-ground power lines should be buried over time until all power infrastructure is underground except in those historically protected areas.

Our lack of preparation and single-minded focus on attacking the oil-and-gas sector has left us in a perfect storm. The climate is changing, and bouts of extreme climate events are increasing. The successive "hottest years on record" require huge amounts of energy for cooling in the summer. Solar energy and wind energy are not currently as reliable as more available sources such as hydro, nuclear, and natural gas. Energy is required to fight flooding in the spring and wildfires in the summer. Cold snaps in Alberta in the winter of 2024 and the great power crisis of 2021 in Texas showed that the electricity grid is unable to keep up with energy demands even with the current levels of fossil fuel usage. Overall energy needs are still increasing, particularly in developing nations. Yet, we are being pushed to purchase electric vehicles and reduce our use of even relatively clean fossil fuels such as natural gas. Wind and solar energy, not to mention EV production require huge amounts of energy themselves for their production, including the mining of rare materials and the outsourcing of components from countries that do not necessarily care about the environment. The boom in artificial intelligence is making enormous energy demands of its own that will cause still further strains on the existing power grid.

The north, our north, is home to vast natural resources and is currently under-protected. Why not seize this opportunity to prosper? The north could be our greatest asset, but the government needs to put the effort into it; it needs a vision for its development. In 2011, the government of Quebec produced its "Plan Nord," a strategy for the development of northern Quebec. Although not perfect, the strategy can provide a model for the environmentally conscious development of Canada's energy, mining, and forestry resources while acknowledging the fact that the climate is indeed changing and that the Northwest Passage may soon be ice-free year-round.

We should embrace First Nations' knowledge of this land, and of the north, and welcome them as key players in our future and the management of resources. Who better to help us regain our sovereignty and to protect it in the north than those who have lived there for centuries? Such a plan also taps into the value of another Canadian resource: respect. Respect for ideas that all Canadians can support regardless of their identity. Respect for our First Nations and their heritage. We must ensure that members of our Indigenous communities have the same opportunities as other Canadians. We must stop over-promising and under-delivering—think of the issue of fresh water on reserves. And we need to acknowledge the harms committed in the past, honestly and forthrightly, but we also need to move forward in a meaningful way.

Our Indigenous people can be our best partners if we have the openness to communicate with them, to be frank and reasonable with them and get the same in return from them, and to treat them as full partners in the development of our country. This will be beneficial to all Canadians.

Climate change mitigation should also account for populations that will migrate northward from those areas that become too hot in the equatorial latitudes. As part of a national security course in Kingston in 1993, my colleagues and I were told by a climatologist that Canada's northern latitude would become more temperate; the instructor had a map showing temperatures in northern Canada becoming less extreme, especially in winter. So, thirty years ago, we knew the climate was changing and had the opportunity to start making preparations and reasonable accommodations. Instead, we've just been ringing alarms and attacking our resource sector. Today, if population migration is going to take place, our country needs to develop laws appropriate to border-crossing caused by climate change, and industry needs to consider opportunities this may bring. For that matter, this may be something practical the UN needs to consider as a part of international law.

The topic of water protection has been one of my worries for many years. As demonstrated during the major watermain break in Calgary in June 2024, a lack of water can affect everyone and even an advanced country like ours needs to protect this essential resource. Singapore, one of the most water-stressed nations in the world, has become a global hub for water technology with over 200 water companies and more than twenty research centres. With all of our reserves, we ought to play a part in this research area and we need to protect our freshwater. I applaud the announcement of the creation of the Canadian Water Agency in 2023 as part of Environment and Climate Change Canada with its headquarters in Winnipeg. What will be important is to ensure the agency remains future focussed and operational, unlike many other public service organisations.

There is a role for electric vehicles in certain sectors of the economy where they can be put to good use, but we will still need fuel-efficient internal combustion and hybrid vehicles. For governments (and automakers) to declare an intention to stop producing gas-burning vehicles by a hard-stop date as early as 2025 is wishful thinking.

Unfortunately, I think the government's obsession with climate change will result in Canada being left behind by the rest of the world's pragmatism. While we try to become greener than anyone, other nations are using fossil fuels to lift their people out of poverty. Our neighbour, the US, has become the world's largest exporter of natural gas—exporting higher volumes even with Democrats in power in Washington. Some months ago, the UK walked back its commitments to meet its net-zero pledge agreed at the EU, and the opposition Labour party supported the government. The British PM approved development of a giant offshore oil and gas field and has reportedly delayed signing off on green policies that would impose "unacceptable costs" to ordinary workers and families.

Our country can return to being a positive force in the world, while helping ordinary Canadians pull themselves out of poverty. It again comes down to developing a vision that all of us can support, that calls for all of us to put our shoulder to the wheel and push in the same direction. It recalls the manner of former premier Frank MacKenna of New Brunswick who, when he assumed power, made two commitments that I admire: one, that he would serve for ten years and no more, and two, that he wanted to focus his time in office on job creation. As he said, the "best social program we have is a job." He had a vision of what his province could be, to the benefit of all New Brunswickers. He then set about realizing this vision by enticing companies to move to NB, going so far at times to personally calling their executives. And he resigned on the tenth anniversary of assuming the premiership.

With a vision for the country that benefits its huge potential and a communication plan to explain it to our citizens, Canadians would get it. On climate change, we can show the way.

CHAPTER 7

The Economy in Crisis

I AM NOT AN ECONOMIST. In fact, my marks in economics courses at RMC were so bad that the faculty agreed to give me a bare pass if I would promise *never* to become an economics major. But as an ordinary Canadian, one of two million whose mortgage is up for renewal this year, I find it impossible not to comment on the current economic trajectory of our country. We could all write chapters and verses on how Canada could take better care of our military, senior citizens, veterans, immigrants, those needing medical care, and the environment, but none of these bright ideas are possible if the country is bankrupt.

Why is our economy in such dire straits? Again, in my opinion, it boils down to a lack of fiscal leadership and responsibility, and the victory of politics over common sense.

The current situation is a result of a government led by someone who by his own admission (in 2021) does "not think about monetary policy" and who genuinely thought the budget would balance itself no matter how much he spent. Out-of-control spending exacerbated by the COVID-19 pandemic were factors that led his finance minister, Bill Morneau, to resign from politics in August 2020 and forced his Bank of Canada governor to quit. Morneau stated later that "policy rationales were tossed aside in favour of scoring political points" and these led to "the largest government expenditures as a portion of GDP . . . in the shortest time since the advent of World War Two." Remember, this was a government that in 2015 inherited a healthy economy.

Before he won the 2015 election, Justin Trudeau promised modest, temporary deficits. Since that promise, according to a 2023 CBC News report, the federal debt grew to "double the $612.3 billion it was when Trudeau and his team took the reins of power." The cost to Canada of servicing this debt in outrageous. In 2023, it cost Canadians $46.5 billion, more money than we spend on the entire defence budget. These funds could and should have been used to make the lives of Canadians better, not gobbled up by interest payments on a reckless national debt. Imagine the beneficial effect of spending $46.5 billion on our seniors, military, or underfunded social programs.

The government itself has grown significantly; the federal public service has 40 percent more employees today than it had in 2015. Although Stephen Harper managed to reduce the federal public service workforce from 283,000 to 257,000 by the time he left office, Trudeau increased that number annually until in 2023, when the Treasury Board indicated the federal public service was 357,247 strong, an increase of over 100,000. Total expenses to run this bloated federal government have increased by $151 billion annually. Yet if you asked Canadians if the services provided by the federal government—think passports, employment insurance, pensions, Canada Revenue Agency, small business grants, and the infamous vaccine rollout—are exponentially better since 2015, the answer would be a resounding no.

The Bank of Canada raised its interest rate to 5 percent in July 2023, and that rate, the highest in over twenty years, is holding steady into 2024 at time of writing. Ostensibly a higher interest rate should bring down inflation. If the cost of borrowing is higher, people will spend less and the demand for goods is reduced, which causes prices to go down, or at least to go up more slowly. Yet inflation has remained high; in 2022, food prices rose by 7.8 percent, rents were up 6.5 percent, and housing prices did not come down, in part because of weak supply. Taxes, like the carbon tax, made a simple trip to the grocery store anything but simple. Unsurprisingly, the government is accepting no blame for this mess but pointing the finger at everyone else: the CEOs of major grocery chains, large corporations, the broken supply chain, the pandemic—the list of blameworthy targets is all-encompassing. The government in Ottawa just can't make the connection to its own thirst for public spending.

The interest rate is of huge significance to a homeowner renewing a mortgage in 2024. In 2019, a five-year fixed-rate $500,000 mortgage could be approved for the average rate of 2.8 percent. This mortgage would have cost the homeowner a monthly payment of $2,315. In early 2024, the average five-year fixed rate is 6.8 percent, and the same mortgage will cost the homeowner a monthly payment of $3,440. To the average Canadian, a $1,000-per-month increase is huge, even disastrous. A telling statistic from Food Banks Canada indicates that more homeowners are accessing food banks than ever before.

When I grew up, an accepted principle of home ownership was that you could afford a house that would cost three times your annual salary. So, if you made $30,000 a year, you could probably afford a $90,000 house. Today, the average salary in Canada is about $65,000. The 33-percent equation allows for a home costing $195,000. But the average price of a home in Canada in 2022, according to Statistica, was $704,000. In urban centres, the price is significantly more. To younger Canadians, the dream of owning a home is fast fizzling. Even for a couple with two good incomes, the current economic climate precludes this once common dream. Soaring interest rates, teamed with high house prices, a drastic shortage of available housing, and uncontrolled immigration mean fewer Canadians will ever be able to afford a home. A Royal Bank of Canada report in December 2023 stated that 45 percent of Canadians currently cannot afford a condo and that only 26 percent can afford a single-family house. One must ask, what does this situation do for the psyche of our young generation? Dim prospects for the future equal a loss of hope.

Affordability of anything—housing, food, transportation—has become a distant memory. The introduction of "just transition" was a body blow to our country's natural resources sector, strangling our industries from fisheries to oil to natural gas. Chemical plants that produce petroleum and plastics, mining of rare earth metals and any company with interests in our oil fields or natural gas are obstructed by the government's environmental gatekeepers; approvals to produce anything are unbelievably difficult to obtain. Even when socially conscious private companies negotiate in good faith with different First Nations and get their approval, special-interest groups can block construction and transportation. Economic hardship and loss of livelihood for millions of Canadians is a sacrifice the government is willing to make at the altar of climate change and other so-called progressive policies.

We are beginning to see that the carbon tax, meant to force Canada into zero emissions, was a bridge too far. Today, many Canadians are wondering if they can afford the gas to drive to a grocery store, the heat to warm their homes, and if there will be enough left of their paycheques to renew their mortgages. The whole carbon tax scheme was meant to discourage consumption of oil and gas, but it has done neither. The scheme lost much of its appeal when the government removed the tax from home heating oil in the Atlantic provinces, which then led to appeals from First Nations to also remove the tax. The carbon tax does nothing for the environment and is, indeed, a tax. As we now have seen, the rebates to those who pay the tax can never match the initial outlay.

The 2024 budget indicated yet another deficit, this to the tune of $40 billion. This amount includes $21 billion on climate initiatives, $17 billion on Indigenous reconciliation, and, of course, the $13 billion on a national dental care program to satisfy the Liberal–NDP coalition of mutual unction. Payments to small special-interest groups and any event or organization that supports a progressive agenda account for hundreds of millions of dollars. According to the Fraser Institute, almost $60 billion has been paid out and continues to be paid out as reparations for the Indigenous residential school's so-called "cultural genocide," yet there are still many First Nations communities that do not have access to fresh water. I would have thought that a few of those billions might have been better spent on ensuring this untenable situation was fixed. It is again a question of priority vs photo op. Subsidies for foreign investment abound, including the EV battery plants to which billions were promised, with no guarantee that our economy will benefit or prosper from this investment. In fact, as reported by the *National Post* in January 2024, the $35 billion in EV subsidies will create, at best, 8,500 jobs. When you do the math, this works out to a cost of $4 million per job.

Canadian productivity is rated in the lower echelons of the thirty-eight nations of the Organization for Economic Co-operation and Development (OECD). The OECD predicted in 2021 that Canada's economy will be the worst performing of all its members over the next decade and for three decades after.

Fraser Institute data shows that prosperity on a per-capita basis has been stagnant since the mid-2010s. A report by Bennett Jones, a Toronto law firm, urged changes in government investment to address the situation. Economist Jack Mintz says, "real GDP per capita has stalled since 2018 and in 2023 it actually fell—by 2.4 percent—and is likely to fall again in 2024." The March 2024 numbers released by Bank of Canada are indeed grim, and the deputy governor called it an emergency—time to "break the glass." In 2022, Canadian productivity (output produced per hour worked) was 71 percent that of the United States, down from 88 percent in 1984, and during this period, Canada fell behind all G7 nations other than Italy. According to a Statistics Canada report in April 2024, Canada's output per capita plummeted 7 percent below its long-term trend: it is a crisis of productivity.

Part of the issue is the low investment of the government in research and development which, if funded properly, would help find new and more efficient ways of doing things. Another reason for our lacklustre performance is the unconstrained immigration of the last few years. An increase in immigrants before they begin contributing to the economy, before they even have a place to live, obviously reduces the per-capita productivity numbers. The alteration of the immigration system is partly to blame, according to the report.

When the government opened the borders to refugees in 2017, declaring Canada a safe haven for those fleeing persecution, terror, and war in response to former US president Donald Trump's executive order on immigration, the floodgates opened. Roxham Road in Quebec became the focal point for unregulated refugee crossings. Countless people entered from the US without being vetted and added an immediate burden to cities and provinces trying to house them and provide health care. In early 2024, municipalities and provinces approached the federal government asking for funding to fix these problems. Toronto sought hundreds of millions of dollars, and the premier of Quebec wrote to the prime minister asking him to restrict the number of arrivals because the province was at a breaking point in terms of housing and education, and in its ability to assimilate newcomers. It is another excellent example of the government's virtue signalling with no thought to second-order effects, actual costs, consequences, or burdens this policy would inflict on Canadians.

As a simple man, I want my government to be fiscally responsible, to live within its means, spending on identified priorities that profit the common good and that ensure increased productivity and growth. At the top of those priorities (and I'm sure you expected this) is the ability for our country to defend itself, to protect our sovereign territory against both internal and external threats, from security concerns to environmental emergencies.

CHAPTER 8

Immigration

I AM NOT AN IMMIGRANT, nor am I from an immigrant family, unless you go back eleven generations. My ancestor, Pierre Maisonneuve, came to New France in the mid-seventeenth century. As far as I know, none of the successive generations of Maisonneuves strayed far from Eastern Ontario, Quebec, or French-speaking Canada. My own parents were decidedly Quebecois, although my father, a Franco-Ontarian born in Rockland, had the courage to perpetually relocate our family to where the jobs were and had us living in Prince Albert, Thunder Bay, and Calgary, to name a few of our stops. Looking back, it was an amazing experience to live and grow in such diverse Canadian landscapes. But to a teenager filled with the usual adolescent angst, it was traumatizing.

My parents were not particularly patriotic in the flag-waving, hand-on-heart way we typically associate with Americans. I'm not sure I thought very deeply about patriotism myself until I donned the Canadian Armed Forces uniform. My oldest brother Claude had served a three-year stint in the army and my parents were very proud of him. When I joined, I believe they were very proud of me as well, and they continued to support me, as did my entire family, throughout my military career. As I look back at my life and my service, I consider myself to be very patriotic, believing that my country and its inhabitants are some of the greatest, most talented, and worthy human beings who ever lived.

The "new world" used to be the term used to describe the western hemisphere lands, most especially the Americas, north and south. The term was coined as far back as the 1500s. But in the nineteenth and twentieth centuries, it meant so much more than that. To Europeans, whose lands had been ravaged by wars, revolutions, famines, plagues, and fallout from the Industrial Revolution, it meant a golden opportunity, a place in which to start over and chase your dreams. To the millions of immigrants who came in search of those dreams, the possibilities were endless. And they came in droves. The term "new world" has fallen out of favour, mostly because it seemed to disregard the First Nations to whom the Americas had been home for thousands of years. I don't think that was the intent—the term was coined long before political correctness became the defining principle of our past, present, and future.

I identify the founding peoples of Canada as First Nations, the French settlers, the British colonists, and immigrants. Through most of our history, immigrants came to Canada with their dreams intact, leaving behind their homelands with a primary goal of becoming Canadian, embracing their new homeland, its values and traditions, and above all chasing the goal of Canadian citizenship.

My wife is a first-generation Canadian. Her parents immigrated to Canada as displaced persons post WW2. My father-in-law was a Ukrainian farmer who was offered immigrant status to Canada from a displaced persons camp in Austria. He thought he had won a lottery and often told me that once he had that paper in hand, he never said another word until he was on board the ship to Halifax, in case it should turn out to be a mistake and he could not leave. That was April 1947.

My mother-in-law's story is slightly different. She was German and a member of the Rommel family, a relative of the legendary German general Erwin Rommel, the fabled Desert Fox. As an armoured (tanker) officer, I found this familial connection impressive. After the war, she worked for the British at the Control Commission Germany in Hannover, West Germany. As the Allies' relationship with the Soviets deteriorated, she was advised to leave Germany. In November 1951, she secured a visa to emigrate to Canada.

It would be difficult for me to find two people more passionate in their love for Canada than my in-laws. I never visited their European hometowns; indeed, my father-in-law never returned to Ukraine. My mother-in-law made the journey back to Germany five times, once every ten years, the last in 2005. The places they spoke of are alive in my mind from the stories they loved to tell. I also loved to hear the stories of their immigration experience: the desire to do well, the pride in making it on their own, and the camaraderie of European immigrants from the early 1950s whose only common thread was the joy of being given the chance to be Canadian. This was crucial: being Canadian was a common goal, akin to winning a jackpot. But what did being Canadian mean to them, and how does that goal seem to differ from many immigrants who come to this country today?

To my in-laws, being Canadian meant everything from speaking English at home to each other and to their children; attending the annual Six Nations pow-wow; patronizing the local farmer's market weekly; and to attempting to figure out our version of football, bafflingly different from European soccer. It meant adopting the Canadian way of celebrating holidays, anniversaries, and traditions. Amusing family stories of the hit-and-miss successes of these early days abounded.

When my mother-in-law first arrived in Hamilton, she visited the downtown market for fresh food. Money was extremely tight, and there wasn't much left over for treats. On her first foray, she came across a farmer selling fresh eggs. It had been months since she'd eaten a fresh egg.

"How much?" she asked.

"Fifty cents," was the reply.

She paused. "That's a lot," she said.

"Well, everything is getting expensive," said the farmer.

My mother-in-law decided to splurge and counted out the fifty cents. The farmer grabbed a bag and started counting out a *dozen* eggs. She stared at him and gasped, "I gave you fifty cents!" To which he replied, "Yes, and I'm giving you a dozen eggs." She thought she was getting only one egg for her hard-earned fifty cents. Imagine her delight! That night at her rooming house on Caroline Street, she and three other girls living there feasted on the best tasting scrambled eggs they ever had.

Ukrainians and Germans celebrate Christmas with specific time-honoured customs. To my father-in-law, Christmas was celebrated on January 6, his Christmas Eve, and the highlight was an hours-long meal that included no less than twelve meatless dishes, heavy on the *pedaheh* (Ukrainians vehemently resist using *pierogi* to describe these boiled dumplings), and lots of fish. To my mother-in-law, Christmas Eve began when the children went to church with their father, during which time their mother decorated the tree and placed beneath its branches gifts which had been left by the Christ child. Both parents cherished these ethnic celebrations but, especially after their children arrived, moved to embrace the Canadian Christmas and all its customs. The idea of Santa Claus coming down the chimney was logistically challenging for them as the family home did not possess a fireplace, but they managed by telling the children that he in fact landed on the second-level balcony, next to the clothesline, and came in through that upper-level door.

Once my wife and her brother started school and met other Canadian kids, more local traditions were embraced. Hallowe'en was particularly difficult for my father-in-law to comprehend. As far as he could make out, children celebrated the day when the dead came back to this world, dressed up in frightening costumes and went door to door, asking for candy. The very idea of imitating the underworld was bad enough, but the festivities made it look like he couldn't afford to buy his children candy so they were forced to go door to door begging the neighbours for treats. It was almost too much to bear.

IMMIGRATION

My in-laws were cognizant of the First Nations and their role in Canada. Always eager to learn about their new homeland, they never missed the annual pow-wow at the Six Nations reserve close to Caledonia, Ontario. Decades later, when I joined the family, I still heard fond anecdotes of those visits and was impressed that their knowledge of the First Nations was as extensive as most Canadians' educated here.

Amusing anecdotes aside, what did Canada represent to these immigrants? Canada represented endless possibilities. If you worked hard, you could do or be anything you wanted. The resources of their new home were countless, a country where you could become successful as a farmer, a fisherman, an oil patch worker, or a miner. There were no pogroms, corrupt state police or party memberships which you had to possess to keep you and your family safe. There was no historical caste system; your children could grow up free and become anything *they* wanted. Being Canadian was the ultimate goal, while ethnicity was welcomed. Everyone could attend the pow-wow or Fest Italia or Oktoberfest. It seems to me that this was inclusivity at its best, and the ideas of cultural appropriation, of oppressor vs oppressed, were thankfully absent.

Becoming a citizen of another country is a giant leap of faith and a frightening proposition for most. Everyone has ties to their homeland, and I know that for my in-laws, many heartstrings felt the tug at times during this journey of truly becoming Canadian. From signing the citizenship application, the final step in renouncing the citizenship of their births, to receiving their first Canadian passport, cheering for Canada while watching the Olympic games, proudly bearing witness as their daughter was sworn into the Canadian Armed Forces—I am sure these events brought more than a few mixed feelings.

But the overriding sentiment, I believe, was the idea that they, as immigrants of that era, came to Canada with no intention of ever going back. They left behind the turmoil and hatred and despair, and they came to Canada to become Canadian forever. Not just to wait out the latest civil war, not to foster the hatred and terrorist ideals here that they were mired in over there, not to impose their culture and religion and political beliefs on the citizens of their new country, but to embrace the Canadian way of life, its value system, and its ideals. They came to contribute to Canada, expecting nothing for free other than the opportunity to be given a fair chance to prosper through hard work and good citizenship.

I don't believe this is what all immigrants come to Canada for today. I believe the shift began with the elder Trudeau, who enacted the multiculturalism policies that encouraged new Canadians to keep their own traditions and culture *above* those of Canadians already here. Much has been made of the dreaded "melting-pot" theory that Americans ascribe to, and we patted ourselves on the back for creating a "mosaic" rather than a melting pot. My fiercely patriotic in-laws did not think much of this policy. In the words of my mother-in-law, the melting pot was not great, but the mosaic was just individual pieces that didn't blend or overlap. They stood alone, separated and individual, rather than making the whole better. Much better to be a big salad bowl, she said. The long-time Canadians were the lettuce, and, of course, you cannot have salad without lettuce. But the salad is much more delicious when you add the Italian sausage, the French cheese, and the Greek dressing. And then you eat it with Moroccan hummus and Korean kimchi on the side. That's Canada!

The concept of multiculturalism has morphed into the post-national state of Justin Trudeau. Once again, the pendulum has swung too far. We have been convinced that our history is shameful. Best to eradicate any mention of it, let alone take pride in it. Even our Canadian passport, which used to show photographs of some of our heroes and our most iconic historic monuments and scenes has been changed to remove any trace of a past. The new Crayola images reflect no tie to a country and no attempt to highlight our wonderful, if at times painful history, or our heroes.

Identity politics have become *de rigueur*, and as Tasha Kheiriddin so aptly stated in a November 2023 piece in the *National Post*, "It was no longer sufficient to call yourself Canadian, or even a hyphenated Canadian; you were encouraged to categorize yourself by privileged/non-privileged, white/non-white, gendered/genderfluid, settler-colonizer/Indigenous and a host of other personal characteristics dreamed up in the halls of academia." She called Canada "a nation of diasporas."

Canada has become a country where shame is the only history—Indigenous residential schools, toppling statues, flag at half-mast for months on end—and where the PM schedules cross-country trips not to extoll our virtues but to apologize for our past. Where any opportunity is seized upon to condemn our founding fathers and veterans and those who made this country great. Where the focus is on special-interest groups. Veterans get one day so we may honour their sacrifice, while LGBTQ2+ get an entire month of parades, classroom lessons, media coverage, even to the point where their flag takes precedence over the red maple leaf.

What must potential immigrants think of this? An immigrant looking to find a new country, to start over, to raise their children in a place of freedom and possibilities—why would they choose Canada?

Today's immigrants are not invited here to help make Canada better, they are encouraged to tick their own boxes. The further removed those boxes are from the values upon which Canada was built, the warmer the welcome. The result is that once they are here, they feel no obligation to become Canadian. On the contrary, they are encouraged to be offended and point fingers at every aspect of Canadian society that doesn't mesh with their ideologies or expectations, confident that pointing out that our Christmas tree makes them feel excluded will result in the removal of the tree.

Some bring their grievances and extremism here and continue to protest *en masse* what they couldn't at home. They remain in a holding pattern until they can return; they attempt to impose their culture on us rather than adopting ours, knowing that this behaviour will be tolerated. They also know that were we to emigrate to their homeland, none of this would be tolerated. We would be forced to adapt and adopt the norms of their culture, and not doing so could result in significant consequences.

The audacity is unchallenged. Canadians have been groomed to apologize and decry the very ideals that made Canada great. The fact that the majority of Canadians today had absolutely nothing to do with the "shame" of our past is irrelevant. We must atone for these alleged or inflated misdeeds of the past at the expense of what made us who we are.

I must point out that not all new Canadians fit this mould. There are still those who view Canada as a land of opportunity, a place where they can come to be Canadian. These hard-working folks are just as dismayed at this post-national state as we are. One Vietnamese immigrant couple that I know, small business owners who managed to keep their business (but not their home) during the pandemic, told me that people who come to Canada should have to learn how to be Canadian. When asked what he meant by that, he said, "Well, in Canada, when you pass someone on the street you are supposed to smile and say hello! That's what we do in Canada!" How refreshing.

Once again, anyone who expresses the view that immigrants should integrate into our country and adopt our values risks being cancelled. Remember *Hockey Night in Canada* icon Don Cherry? He was cancelled for expressing the view that everyone should wear the poppy during Remembrance Week. That is one of the things that make us Canadian: wearing the poppy to remember those we lost in wars and conflicts where Canadians stood up to defend the country and our values. Cherry should have been applauded.

My view is simple. Canada was built on Judeo-Christian values; these are still good values. They emphasize acceptance, forgiveness, equality, reward for hard work, and democracy. It is common sense that the laws must apply to all citizens, and not be modified for special-interest groups or minorities. It is not okay to burn down churches and then be told by your government that "it is understandable." It is *not*.

Nor is it okay for Canadian Jews to be afraid to venture outside or be harassed daily by a mob spouting distinctly un-Canadian sentiments. Or for people to come here and demand that our Christmas trees be removed. It is not OK for our government to dismantle our culture and then appeal to the very Canadian values that they scorn when caught in the crosshairs of the discontent their policies created.

It is time for Canadians to speak out and demand our country back. It is time to revise our immigration policy so that it is designed to make Canada better. It should not be a refuge for illegal aliens, extremists, and those who use our country as a platform to continue their homelands' political struggles. The very notion that Canada can welcome someone for whom Interpol has issued two red notices ("a request to law enforcement worldwide to locate and provisionally arrest a person pending extradition, surrender, or similar legal action"), or who is on the terrorist list of an allied country—even allowing that person to engage in militant activities here—is absurd and dangerous. Immigrants need to be vetted; they should have to prove that their presence in Canada will improve Canada. And if they are found conducting illegal activities here before they are naturalized, they should be deported.

In November 2023, Leger conducted a poll of 1,531 Canadians over the age of eighteen and asked specific questions on Canadian diversity and the role that diversity plays in our immigration policies. The answers surprised, I think, a lot of people. More than that, the answers should have affected the government's stance on diversity above all else:

- 78 percent of respondents were concerned over the Gaza–Israel conflict and its impact on Canadian communities.
- 51 percent of Canadians believe the government should do more to ensure newcomers accept Canadian values.
- The majority of Canadians believe that diversity is not the success story hailed by the media and our leaders.
- 56 percent agreed with the statement that "some elements of diversity can provide strength, but some elements can cause problems and conflict in Canada."
- As far as giving certain minority groups additional rights and privileges

in accordance with the notions of decolonization, anti-racism, and equity towards the goal of addressing historical wrongs, 50 percent do not agree with the practice. Only 24 percent agree, and the rest don't know.

The results of this poll indicate Canadians (the silent majority) are not happy with the current plan of immigration for everyone and immigration at all costs. The massive immigration targets Canada has set are detrimental to the country. There is no better way to create a post-national state than to flood the country with millions of immigrants who are not required to become Canadian, not required to learn our history, adopt our culture, or even speak one of our official languages. This is clearly not what Canadians want. The government needs to start listening to its own citizens about how their immigration policies are affecting the population. So-called diversity is not fostering inclusion or tolerance. It is having the opposite effect: it is pitting neighbours against each other, causing serious harm to our economy, and it is hurting Canada as a whole. Our social fabric is strained, as are critical civil needs like housing, health care, education, and social services. This is unsustainable and Canadians are suffering.

We need to change direction. A quid pro quo contract with anyone wishing to become a Canadian must be established: immigrants must give something in return for the privilege of living here. The goal should not be to swell the population numbers to provide the government with gratitude votes, it should be to induce people with something to offer the opportunity to come here and contribute to our society. Merely checking the DEI box or meeting a quota is not enough. Becoming Canadian used to be a lofty goal; it should be so again.

Before that is possible, Canada has to reclaim its status as a place that offers opportunity, economic success, and freedom. No one wants to come to a bankrupt country. We need to rebuild our reputation in the world, remove the image of a country that places no value on national security, history, economic freedom, and hard work. It's time to eliminate radical progressivism and become proud of who we are and what our country stands for. Only then will we attract people who want to be Canadian and who will value this nation and all the opportunities it offers.

CHAPTER 9

The Military

WE ARE LIVING IN one of the most complex, dangerous, and unpredictable times in human history. We are witnessing increasing global instability and a broader range of threats, now state-on-state as well as from non-state actors. The world will not become less complex or more predictable. Three years ago, no one could have predicted the COVID-19 pandemic, a war in Europe, or the bloody attack by Hamas on Israel and its justified response. The only way for Canada to manage these new complexities, each seemingly more challenging than the preceding one, is to be better prepared to meet them. Unfortunately, our military is woefully unprepared, even though national security and the defence of democratic values are more important than ever.

The rapid development of information technology, cyber warfare, quantum computing, and artificial intelligence seems to be the enabling force of the new strategic environment, having propelled us from the industrial age beyond the information age. This explosion not only increases the efficiency of delivering force, but also increases the efficiency of those who seek to do grave harm. Drones and unmanned aerial and land weapons are proliferating, with commercial, inexpensive, off-the-shelf solutions being offered to military and unconventional forces. The international and domestic regulations required to harness and control these new developments lag behind, which leads to their unbridled use by individuals and states with the potential to do harm. Canada and other nations must therefore structure, organize, equip, train, educate, and fund their forces and capabilities to capitalize on the new innovations, while preparing to counter the threats they pose.

Canada's top operational military commander, Vice-Admiral Bob Auchterlonie, stated in December 2023, "We are in the middle of this and I'm not sure everybody understands that the security and defence situation globally has deteriorated significantly." The international security situation should be a source of worry even for us Canadians who have long believed we lived in a "fireproof house." We do not view these threats as ones that can directly target Canada. That is a mistake.

It is well known that four nations sit atop the list of states most dangerous to global peace: Russia, China, Iran, and North Korea. Since 9/11, we have seen a proliferation of non-state actors and terrorists. My friend Rick Hillier, Canada's former chief of defence staff, called them "despicable murderers and scumbags." These include Hamas, the Iranian Republican Guard Corps, ISIS or ISIL, and lone wolves operating with evil intentions, all of whom continue to threaten our way of life.

The world is in a precarious state. Russia showed its true colours by invading Ukraine in February 2022. China is dangerous on multiple fronts with its desire to expand its empire, reclaim Taiwan, and disrupt marine activity in the South China Sea. India and Pakistan continue to flex their newfound (nuclear-armed) muscles, and Israel, the only democracy in the Middle East and Canada's friend and ally, is in the midst of a war with Hamas, a terrorist organization. After the killing of three American soldiers and the wounding of thirty more in a drone attack in Jordan in January 2024, the US and UK have begun retaliatory strikes on targets in Iraq, Syria, and the Iran-backed Houti rebels that have been attacking commercial ships in the area.

Some European nations are returning to conscription to be better prepared to face the threat of conflict. Even UK and German politicians have floated the idea of conscription or national service in the face of an unsettled global security situation. Other nations, including France, are using the idea of national service to ensure citizens are aware of the responsibilities that come with the privilege of citizenship.

Cyber threats, hybrid threats, disinformation, and the rise of artificial intelligence are having an impact on the information we receive and can also sow doubt in institutions that were once highly respected. As we saw with the suspected Chinese interference in our elections, and the cavalier way former governor-general David Johnston dealt with the issue, our complacency and lack of outrage continue to be apparent. And the issue of foreign interference in Canadian political affairs appears to be more prevalent than initially thought.

It is obvious as well that we are sorely lacking in international leadership and statesmanship. As a former chief of staff at one of NATO's two strategic commands, I was astounded that no action was taken when Russia annexed Crimea in 2014. It was a typical approach by Vladimir Putin: act and see what the reaction is. Putin probably thought, "Will the world react to my so-called referendum? Do people care about this part of a nation that used to belong to the USSR? Are there leaders out there, particularly in NATO, who will stand up to my aspirations to recreate the Soviet empire?" We answered "no" to all of those questions, so it turned out Putin was right: that no state would object beyond levying some sanctions coupled with a lot of cheap talk. NATO cancelled the NATO–Russia Council and tried to isolate Russia, ignoring the adage "Keep your friends close and your enemies closer." In total, it was a lackadaisical response to an important crisis that emboldened Putin.

After seeing the lack of action or desire by the West to come to Ukraine's defence in 2014, Putin gambled that he could go to war and successfully invade all of Ukraine eight years later in his "special military operation." That move resurrected familiar chestnuts of the Cold War, including concepts such as the domino effect and the fighting of proxy wars. And so, our leaders decided they would fight this war to the last Ukrainian.

If we care about Canadian values, we should care about the erosion of those values internationally. If Canadians want to be good global citizens, we should care that other nations are being swallowed up by illiberal states led by criminals and dictators. We cannot continue to stand by and let the next dominoes fall. Taiwan? The slice of Ukraine the Russians hold already? What about our own north and the Northwest Passage? At this point, we have neither the capability nor the leadership to do anything about outstanding threats. Even though the government has committed to upgrade our participation in NORAD, we are a very junior member, and I am sure US leaders are fed up with our posturing, hand-wringing and lack of defence spending. Only direct pressure by our southern neighbour forced the government to spend on NORAD upgrades at all, and we still refuse to join the Ballistic Missile Defence parameters.

* * *

I was lucky to serve as the principal aide-de-camp to a great Canadian, an eminent historian, and one of the people behind the design of the Canadian flag, Colonel the Honourable Dr. George F. G. Stanley, while he served as the lieutenant governor of New Brunswick. He wrote a book, aptly titled *Canada's Soldiers: The Military History of an Unmilitary People*. How right he was that Canadians are an unmilitary people. National security has remained low on the priority list of the government because it is far from the mind of Canadians in general. The last time Canada's armed forces were adequately funded, equipped, and staffed was WW2, when the country boasted the world's third largest navy and the fourth largest air force, and had mobilized 1.15 million troops. Since then, the Canadian Armed Forces have fallen into embarrassing disrepair and are able to meet only the most modest commitments.

Canadian governments as far back as Pierre Trudeau's have neglected the military forces of Canada. He was pressured by allies to replace our old Centurion tanks (on which I trained) with Leopard 1s. He did purchase new CF-18 fighter aircraft to satisfy our NORAD responsibilities. But he reduced our commitment in Europe and eventually the fall of the Berlin Wall spelled the end of our two major forward-deployed bases in Germany, one in Lahr and the other in Baden. Brian Mulroney's government, we hoped, would be more supportive of the military. His 1987 white paper, "Challenge and Commitment," was an excellent blueprint drafted by Defence Minister Perrin Beatty. As a staff officer at army headquarters at that time, I was tasked to write the commander's plan—Lieutenant-General Jim Fox—for implementation of the white paper over the next fifteen years, called "Army 2002." Sadly, the money required to implement it never materialized and in April 1989 the plan was ripped up. The priority of Mulroney's successor, Jean Chrétien, was cutting the deficit through "Program Review II," and Finance Minister Paul Martin was his knife. Stephen Harper, although he had promised to restore funding, also allowed cuts to the budget. The result is that, since the dying days of the Cold War, no government has supported or left the defence budget unscathed. The Canadian Armed Forces have languished and continue to do so.

The chief of defence staff and the deputy minister of National Defence, in a message to the department in late 2023, announced there will be reductions in the defence budget over the next three years. What a time for our government to impose further cuts on an already meagre budget and at a time when the CAF are facing a crisis. Unfortunately, as always, Canadians didn't blink an eye. The defence policy update in April 2024 had some good ideas, but pushed most of the funding to the out years and did not commit to protecting the current defence budget; it remains discretionary. Since then, the CDS has been reported to be "confused" about the cuts imposed in late 2023 and the increases announced in the update, saying it is like being asked to "suck and blow at the same time." What a way for the government to treat its armed forces.

THE MILITARY

The issue for successive governments is that, as Max Hastings states, "there are no votes in defence." Security and sovereignty are not usually on the list of issues that preoccupy Canadians. On the other hand, no government has ever made the point cogently to Canadians that security and sovereignty are important with a commensurate need for strong armed forces. This again requires leadership and a government that does not lead with polls, but that develops a vision for the country and then sells that vision. Only then is there a chance that government will fund the military appropriately.

The military is like an insurance policy: if you don't pay your premiums, you will not be covered when an accident happens. Even for domestic operations such as fighting fires or floods, Canada needs military units ready to deploy. The time to look after the military is *before* it is needed because when the crisis happens, it is too late. The difficulty is and has always been that Canadians will always trade military funding for social program funding. Any government that would propose prioritizing military spending would immediately lose support. But I am positive that Canadians would understand the need for balance since no social programs would be possible if our nation was invaded by another power or if our way of life was threatened. You can have butter *and* guns.

* * *

The military—being in the service of one's country—used to be a highly regarded profession. Members of the armed forces were respected and appreciated, although often left in the background unless a crisis brought them to the fore.

Today, the idea of serving in our armed forces gets little traction with the public. It seems the moral contract under which our military personnel serve is broken. CAF members are holding up their end of the agreement: they agree to serve in the defence of our country, sometimes in the harshest conditions for many weeks or months on end. Think of a sailor in January in the North Atlantic when the seas are rough and the ship is iced over, away from family, friends, and the safety of home as they patrol our coasts. Think of a soldier projecting our Canadian values for months at a time in far-away lands, in 50-degree Celsius heat, carrying thirty-kilogram packs, and under the threat of adversaries without honour. Think of a pilot who may have to fly unending missions until they are totally exhausted from the G-forces that pull on their aircraft as they patrol the skies in support of our international commitments and the protection of our sovereignty, only to be buzzed by Russian or Chinese bogies. Or think of our special forces personnel, with the highest level of readiness of any in our military, sometimes at what we call "an hour's notice-to-move." This means from the time the alarm is sounded, they have one hour to be prepared to deploy. They rescue hostages and usually deploy under the greatest secrecy without telling their families where and for how long they are gone. All are quite simply heroes, and most are unknown to average Canadians.

Our men and women in uniform accept their duty to face difficult situations in dangerous places to protect our country, to project Canadian values and to fulfil our commitments to our allies. And they do this while knowing that their life may be in danger. They understand also that they must be willing to give their lives if required to do so; or they may have to ask their subordinates to put *their* lives in danger. That is their part of the moral contract, what they sign up for when they join the CAF; it is what is called the unlimited liability clause. No other profession has this clause in its contract.

Canada and Canadians are the other party to the moral contract. In fulfilling their end, Canadian society also has duties and responsibilities, most importantly to provide the military with all it requires to be as successful as it can be in its mission. This responsibility includes ensuring our forces have the state-of-the-art tools they need, the best leadership, and the best education and training. The contract doesn't end when their careers end; it also demands we look after them when they come home and transition to civilian life.

THE MILITARY

Canada is failing on those obligations and has been failing for many years. For Canadians generally, the armed forces are not important until there is a crisis, and successive governments' support of the forces reflect that mindset. Our troops who have dedicated their lives to serve this country deserve better.

I have incredible admiration and respect for the young men and women who serve our country. They are the best of Canada, but Canada is not giving them the opportunity to be the best they can be. As they constantly did for me, they surprise with their energy, their enthusiasm, their initiative, and their ability; there is nothing they cannot do given the proper tools. They follow in the footsteps of our veterans, from the WW2's "greatest generation" through the Korean war, countless peacekeeping missions, and Afghanistan. They are our insurance policy, and they need Canada to uphold its end of the moral contract.

Finally, there is also the fact that our military is indeed the service of last resort. General John De Chastelain was our chief of defence staff during the Oka crisis in 1990. The government of Quebec had requested support from the CAF to support the police in the standoff. I was in command of my regiment at the time and watching a press briefing. At one point, de Chastelain was asked what would happen if the CAF were not successful. The CDS soberly replied, "We *will* be successful, because after us there is nothing . . ." He was warning everyone that the CAF were the last resort and if we were not successful, there was no one else you could call on to re-establish order. It was a lesson to me as I was preparing to deploy with my regiment to a UN peacekeeping mission in Cyprus.

The social or moral contract is, in my mind, neither appreciated nor understood by Canadians and their government. And if it is understood, it is not being fulfilled.

* * *

By now everyone is aware of the many sexual misconduct issues that have plagued the Canadian military. I do not argue that there have been problems, and I believe we need to find the perpetrators and punish them to the fullest extent of the law. It is not unreasonable to point out that the culture of sexual misconduct is hardly limited to the military. All organizations face similar issues. However, the military, with its strict and formal chain of command, with its own system of punishment and progression, and with its hermetically sealed communications culture, was a place where bad actors could exist and thrive. Those in positions of authority could take advantage of others, and those who were assaulted had difficulty blowing the whistle. As the proportion of women in the CAF increased, a few men were unable or unwilling to change their behaviour. These men and these mindsets are the target of the mandated "culture change" currently ongoing in the CAF.

The whole tilting of society towards progressive politics, including critical race theory and the precepts of DEI, has unfortunately seeped into the CAF. It is also affecting other nations' militaries and has been challenged there as well. The idea of oppressive white supremacists being out of control in the military is being perpetuated by the mainstream media, and the military's professional journals are openly promoting this mindset. Here too, I believe the pendulum has swung too far. Being white, male, and sporting a CAF uniform has become equated with being sexist and racist, bringing an expectation that you personally are the same and need to atone for the sins of the past, regardless of any real or perceived guilt. It is preposterous.

Rarely discussed is the fact that the CAF have been doing the work of eliminating discrimination in the ranks for many decades. I was serving at NDHQ in the 1980s when the first messages about harassment were published; they emphasized that the CAF needed to respect all persons regardless of their race, gender, or sexual orientation. They were a powerful message that was ahead of what other nations were doing in their armed forces at the time. I was proud to see the next step, when all military positions were opened to women, including serving on submarines. When I served as executive assistant to the chief of defence staff, General Maurice Baril, I remember him saying to me that removing barriers to women in the military is only a first step. Making them feel welcome was still required, and we were not there yet.

In the 1990s, mandated programs such as SHARP (Standards for Harassment and Racism Prevention) were put in place. They showed that the CAF recognized there was a need for a change in culture considering the changing norms of society and that the forces were making an effort involving all members.

Following the *Maclean's* investigation ("Rape in the Military") in 1998, which revealed that a series of women had been sexually assaulted while in service, several initiatives emerged: senior officers were criminally charged; the CDS's Operation Honour (an accountability framework) was introduced; and the Deschamps report into sexual misconduct was released as were the Morris Fish report on military justice reform and the Arbour study of sexual misconduct. The scrutiny and the proliferation of studies acknowledged that serious issues within the CAF had indeed existed. It was important and necessary work.

Sadly, it is the nature of these reports and investigations that they focus entirely on negative experiences. They tended to leave the impression that our armed forces were populated by horrible, racist, Neanderthal men. There were few interviews with the many serving women whose experiences had been nothing but positive and who found the men with whom they served in operations honourable and respectful. This isn't to deny that instances of sexual misconduct occurred—that is a fact—but I am convinced that the great majority of men serving in the armed forces today are in fact respectful and decent humans. I have met many serving women who never experienced unwanted advances or, if they did, acted themselves or were supported by peers before the transgressions deteriorated into true assault or other misconduct. Many of these women who were treated equitably in the CAF are frustrated by how some of the more zealous reformers are characterizing the men in the forces.

My wife Barbara counts herself as one of these women. She served for over twenty years in the CAF, initially in the male-dominated military police as a private, the most junior of all ranks. After a successful four years at our military colleges, she became an officer in the logistics branch. She has a multitude of stories of being the only woman in the Jeep, or on the plane, or in the tent. She described being alone in Phnom Phen, Cambodia's capital, with only our small contingent of combat engineers, all male, and in Haiti, where our soldiers and our American allies provided much needed security.

For fifteen months, she was one of the few female officers serving and living with male colleagues on the ceasefire line between Israel and Syria on the Golan Heights. None of these experiences included any kind of sexual harassment or abuse. She speaks fondly of the friendships formed and the experiences shared. My wife does not deny the victims of assault—believe me, she would be the first to lead the charge to prosecute the perpetrators—but she also expresses anger at the rush to judgement after accusations surface. Evidence and due process are essential parts of any investigation and sometimes seem to be lacking.

Again, the #MeToo movement and the hunt for those responsible for abuse was overdue and necessary, but the crusade lacked a process for determining guilt or innocence. There have been too many men accused and ruined by accusations carried in media reports that were later found to be unfounded or insubstantial. The headlines named the accused, but failed to follow up when charges were dropped due to a lack of evidence. The only narrative in these cases belongs to the victim, real or not. Sadly, there were no reparations provided to the men who were unjustly targeted. Their careers were over, their lives ruined, and ultimately, we lost excellent leaders.

In 2018, Barbara was invited as guest of honour to speak at the annual Cadet Mess Dinner at Royal Military College Saint-Jean. Her speech addressed many of these thoughts and was applauded by the staff and cadets at the college, most especially the young female cadets. Unsurprisingly, the speech was attacked by academics and a media personality who implied she did not "believe the women." More thick-skinned than most, she offered to speak to her detractors "after they had walked a mile in my combat boots."

Cultural change is important in any institution, and it is never easy. The cultural change in the Canadian Armed Forces since I signed up has been enormous. Historically, the orderly application of military force up to and including deadly force has been the purview of men. That is no longer the case—a positive development. Who are men to place obstacles in front of women who wish to serve in any military capacity? My view has always been that if a woman wants to serve, and she *meets the standards* for her particular trade, then the door should be wide open for her.

I know a lot of men who are not interested in serving in the infantry, and it's understandable: slogging it on foot with heavy packs in all types of weather in the presence of the enemy, sometimes in a kill-or-be-killed milieu, is not for everyone. But if a woman wants to do it and can do it, why would anyone tell her she cannot? Would we tell a man he cannot? These comments also apply to anyone from the LGBTQ2+ community who should not only be "allowed" to serve but be welcomed and treated with respect—and they in turn should treat others with respect. The new inclusivity of the CAF does mean an adjustment in leadership approach and is a new challenge for military leaders of today. Leadership is still the key and some of the old-school rigid methods that existed in the past no longer apply.

History and tradition are issues that must be considered carefully when it comes to evaluating and modifying culture. History does not change despite those who want to rewrite it. But history must be understood in the context of the era, appreciated (not necessarily agreed with) and learned from, not destroyed. As one of my colleagues stated, traditions should not make up for a lack of initiative. Courageous young men and women within our CAF have that initiative: they can be real agents of cultural change. My personal experience with happy hours, for example, showed me that even in 1990, fitness-focused young officers and soldiers were beginning to change their attitudes towards alcohol and fitness, eschewing the former for the latter.

At this point, we must ensure all these culture change efforts do not supersede the imperative of military effectiveness. Culture change is necessary, but adjusting to new imperatives does not require us to abandon our past and tear down the entirety of our existing culture. The CAF are the protectors of our sovereignty and the defenders of our values. Leading our military forces in today's world with the woke trends that permeate our society is a huge challenge for young officers and non-commissioned members. All of the investigations and reports and subsequent media coverage have painted everyone in the CAF with the same negative brush. They have hurt the morale of those serving, as the chaplain-general of the CAF reported in 2023. Without denying that failures occurred, it is time to acknowledge that the vast majority of men and women in the CAF have served honourably and without incident. It is time to stop the self-flagellation.

* * *

Former prime minister Lester B. Pearson was presented the Nobel Peace Prize in 1957 for his initiative as Canada's external affairs minister to solve the Suez Crisis of the preceding year. In doing so, he developed the concept of UN peacekeeping: the idea of deploying international forces between warring factions to discourage fighting while political solutions could be found.

That moment signalled a sea-change in how many Canadians viewed our role in the world. Before Pearson's Nobel, we punched above our weight militarily and were known for our excellence in land, sea, and air operations. Since Pearson's Nobel, Canadians have fallen in love with the concept of peacekeeping, to the point that Canada contributed to *all* peacekeeping missions during the Cold War, a commitment that involved thousands of our personnel. In the span of little more than a decade, we went from a country with its own landing beach on D-Day, the third largest navy in the world, and known as the home of some of the best planes and pilots in history, to using our military to prevent others from fighting. That sentiment moderated a bit with the advent of the war in Afghanistan, as Canada moved from providing forces to peacekeeping missions to sending war-fighting units in support of NATO, to the chagrin of some Canadians.

There are two issues here that need mentioning. The first is that peacekeeping missions are extremely dangerous, perhaps not as dangerous as war-fighting missions, but they are still unpredictable and, in some ways, more delicate and complex than direct actions against a recognizable enemy. By comparison, Canada lost 159 soldiers during the Afghanistan conflict from 2001 to 2011, while about 130 were lost in peacekeeping missions of all types from 1956 to today. The dangers of peacekeeping missions stem often from the complex nature of the conflict and the difficulties of recognizing the adversary, akin to what has been described by a former UK general as "war among the people."

My first three UN missions consisted of a "traditional" interposition mission between two warring factions in Cyprus, where Greek Cypriots (supported by Greece) were (and still are) facing off against Turkish forces. The Canadian contingent occupied the most sensitive sector of the "green line" which separated the Turkish zone in the north from the Greek-Cypriot zone in the south, running through Cyprus' capital, the old city of Nicosia. This particular conflict is described as traditional because the belligerents are relatively stable, and the interposed peacekeepers have usually been able to keep incidents from degenerating into open fighting. This is not to say the mission is not dangerous.

In my time in theatre, young Canadian soldiers would patrol on foot without helmets and flak vests, carrying a radio between two adversaries facing off across a five-metre-wide street in the centre of Nicosia. Each side had constructed bunkers and reinforced windows of houses with sandbags, complete with firing slits, as they observed the other side and the UN patrols walking by. Yelling insults or rock throwing, incidents that could degenerate into a firefight, would if possible be calmed down by the young soldier on the scene. It was an awesome and dangerous responsibility. The approach was to deal with the incident as low on the chain of command as possible: if the private on the ground could defuse the situation and ensure a return to the status quo, all the better. As I declared to media at the time, these soldiers were doing more for peace that any activist carrying a sign marching on Parliament Hill. If the soldiers could not resolve the issue, it would make its way up the chain until it could be resolved, usually through negotiation.

My last UN mission was in the former Yugoslavia, where I served as the chief operations officer (COO) for the UN Protection Force (UNPROFOR) with the rank of colonel. The mission there was to protect the movement of humanitarian aid convoys serving the people of the new republics of Croatia, Bosnia-Herzegovina, and FYROM (at the time the Former Yugoslav Republic of Macedonia). The 30,000 troops from more than thirty-eight nations that served in this theatre faced danger every day. Canada was providing two complete battlegroups for a total of more than 2,000 personnel. One group was deployed near Sarajevo, the capital of Bosnia and Herzegovina, and the other within Croatia. The conditions of service within this mission were extremely difficult: the rules of engagement were restricted; the belligerents were hardened and well equipped former Yugoslav National Army personnel; there were constant incidents of ethnic cleansing, internally displaced persons, countless checkpoints, undisciplined weapons discharges, and huge civilian strife for the ordinary people caught in the conflict.

I remember our force commander, French General Jean Cot, asking me rhetorically several times, "why are you Canadians here?" He could understand Europeans taking part in the mission, but what were Canadians doing there and in such strength. Canada had been asked to contribute troops; we mattered, and we were engaged across the globe because we had credibility, influence, and courage. We not only lost twenty-three lives in this very dangerous mission, but many brave Canadians came back with injuries, both physical and mental.

The second issue is the reason Canada is so good at peacekeeping: our forces had a reputation as excellent warfighters. Highly trained, well-led, and decently equipped, Canadians had the reputation of being outstanding troops, as demonstrated in WW2, Korea, and more recently Afghanistan. So, in a peacekeeping mission, when things were stable, Canadian UN troops patrolled without personal armour. When situations deteriorated and the warring factions saw Canadians don their helmets and flak vests, they knew we were prepared to intervene to maintain the peace using more than just regular patrolling. Belligerents would think "Uh oh, the Canadians are putting their helmets on, it must be serious. We'd better settle down." It was another way of showing leadership and encouraging adversaries to resolve differences peacefully on the ground. We had a great reputation, and our presence was invaluable to the missions.

Canadians need to understand these two issues. It is all fine and good to be effective peacekeepers and to contribute to the UN, but unless Canada has capable military forces able to defend our country in a wartime scenario, protect its citizens and contribute to international military warfighting missions, our ability to act as peacekeepers will be restricted, and our reputation will suffer.

A colleague, Dr. Walter Dorn, who I consider the foremost Canadian academic authority on UN peacekeeping, told me there are places where Canada could provide troops in a peacekeeping role today if we had the capability. They include the Central African Republic, the UNDOF on the Golan Heights between Syria and Israel (where my wife served for fifteen months when Canada provided the logistics battalion for thirty-two years before pulling out in 2006), or the UN mission in South Sudan, an effort to keep the Sudanese civil war from spilling over into Darfur.

Dorn maintains that before Canada can provide forces to UN peacekeeping missions, our troops need to relearn the lessons of working with the UN, especially our senior personnel who might deploy and need to deal with UN headquarters in New York. I can certainly attest to that. As Lieutenant-General Roméo Dallaire, General Maurice Baril, or Major-General Lewis MacKenzie might tell you, the labyrinthian structure of the UN is not the most reactive problem-solving institution, especially when faced with a crisis. Nevertheless, many peacekeeping missions have succeeded, and Canada could contribute effectively if our forces were in better shape. Although I am critical of the current state of the UN, with its singular focus on climate change and inability to deal with terrorist organizations, I still believe in the potential effectiveness of peacekeeping missions in the right situation.

* * *

Readiness of our CAF means the ability to undertake missions and tasks in support of government objectives. A Department of National Defence report stated in early 2024 that the state of readiness of the CAF showed 50 percent of the equipment was unserviceable with crews unavailable to man it. It's all fine to announce a new Indo-Pacific strategy, but that strategy is useless if we do not have the means to implement it.

All CAF units are assigned a readiness level. The higher the readiness, the shorter the time it takes to deploy. Our highest readiness force is Joint Task Force 2 (JTF2), the special forces unit I mentioned earlier, which is prepared for hostage rescue and other high-priority missions. JTF2 members can deploy within minutes of being called upon. For obvious reasons, the readiness of that specific unit will be protected at all costs. Other forces are at a lower level of readiness but must still be able to deploy. I can attest to the incredible capability of JTF2 soldiers. In the mid 1990s, on a visit to the unit as a colonel, I was asked to play the "hostage" while they rehearsed their rescue capabilities. My captors were represented by two man-sized cardboard targets a few centimetres on each side of the chair I sat in wearing safety glasses and hearing protection. When the door to the training room blew inwards, four members of JTF2 (called "assaulters") burst in, fired live rounds at the head of each target and hustled me out to a waiting helicopter hovering above the roof. Needless to say, I obeyed the order "not to move" I was given before the scenario began. The assaulters presented me with the two targets each with four holes in the head at the mess after the exercise. I was impressed.

Chief of Defence Staff General Wayne Eyre stated in 2023 that he was "concerned about our overall readiness." These words were spoken by a man used to doing the best he could with the little he is given—what we called in my time in the army a "can-do" attitude. Other senior officers also sounded the alarm: the commander of the Royal Canadian Navy published a video that detailed how dire the situation was in the senior service. And the commander of the Canadian Joint Operations Command, what we called the top operator in the CAF, has also decried the state of our forces, in particular the difficulty of dealing with emergencies at home while conducting international operations without enough resources.

Canadians expect the CAF to come to their assistance within Canada, as they should. But sometimes the use of the CAF in domestic operations has an impact on readiness because there are just not enough personnel to handle all potential scenarios. Some of those domestic operations also do not need the CAF, and our troops should only be used as the last resort. These events, like fighting wildfires and containing floods produced by extreme weather, will likely continue in the future. So, our forces need to be sufficiently robust to undertake these domestic missions while still protecting our sovereignty and security and contributing to international stability.

There are many issues that can degrade readiness, such as lack of personnel, lack of equipment, lack of training, and lack of leadership. We can deduce the state of readiness of our forces by examining each of those factors, both individually and how they intersect with each other.

First, personnel. Units are structured for optimal efficiency and success. A unit that loses 15 percent of its personnel is deemed officially combat ineffective in wartime. Our CAF, regular and reserve, is comprised of about 100,000 positions. Reports show 16,500 positions are unfilled, and the CDS has said the requirement of new equipment coming online in the future will require closer to double that figure. So, on average, you could say that right at this moment, we are missing 16 percent of our personnel and that therefore, our forces are currently combat ineffective.

The issue is not only the sheer number of missing personnel; it's also the type of personnel. Those who leave the CAF are usually of mid-level rank, officers or non-commissioned members, who were trained over many years. New and raw recruits, if you can get them, will be unable to fill the empty slots for many years. Specific trades people and specialists, such as pilots, technicians, and engineers, are often the ones who leave because they are highly sought by civilian firms, which pay much higher wages and provide state-of-the-art equipment and training. The impact on unit readiness of missing personnel is, therefore, even greater than the percentage shows.

The number of troops in our units is dangerously low. For example, an infantry battalion would normally be composed of four infantry companies of about 120 each, plus support companies with weapons and services, for a total of about 800 personnel. Today's battalions are structured with a large number of positions unfilled (called "restricted") so that any operational mission undertaken will require a huge amount of reinforcement from other units or the reserves.

Secondly, with respect to equipment, if you are using old pistols or your tank or ship or aircraft spends more time in the shop than operating, your readiness will suffer. This is where we are today. A lack of operational equipment makes it difficult to function in any scenario. Our submarines spend more time in repair shops than at sea. A huge percentage of our land fleet is undergoing repair at any given time, with some estimates of *90 percent* unable to operate. Our troops are forced to buy their own protective equipment. Our air force is eagerly awaiting new fighters, as it has been for years. I could go on. The problem is often spare parts and more importantly the technicians needed to carry out repairs and maintenance. There are hundreds of projects in the pipeline to replace old or obsolete equipment, but deficiencies in the procurement process and lack of funding means even when we secure new equipment, it does not get to the troops in time.

Third, training it is divided into individual training and collective training. Individual training is undertaken at CAF schools and within units. CAF schools have never been fully manned, so they need reinforcement from different units in heavy training periods, thus taking mid-level non-commissioned officers away from their unit for long periods of time.

In collective training exercises, forces learn how to operate, how to fight, and how to win. Training must be as realistic as possible, using real scenarios, and this training must take place before crises occur. Training impacts all personnel and all levels of leadership. It is developed in graduated phases until we reach the highest level of interoperability, including working with allies. Insufficient personnel numbers, faulty equipment, and lack of funding can completely derail training. In today's conflicts, Canada will never operate alone so not only must the CAF excel in their readiness and capability through realistic training at home, but they must also be able to integrate seamlessly into multinational organizations. There is a significant loss of teamwork, credibility, and camaraderie that occurs each time the CAF are forced to stay home. And it happens all too often.

In May 2024, Murray Brewster of CBC reported that the army had decided that our troops who would deploy to Latvia would now do so without having completed the highest level of training and evaluation. The military would now accomplish this last phase of their training in theatre, alongside allies. This is an example of the inability of the CAF to fully operationalize its units and training establishments because of a lack of personnel, equipment, or technicians. What used to be a distinct advantage of CAF units (their high state of training and immediate availability to fight on arrival in theatre) will no longer apply and will reduce their deterrent value, not to mention jeopardize the entire mission.

There are multiple examples of Canada's inability to contribute to international exercises for the reasons stated above. One recent example: in 2023, Canada did not participate in Air Defender, NATO's largest-ever air force exercise involving 10,000 troops and 250 aircraft from 25 nations. Our RCAF pilots lost a rare and precious opportunity to train with other NATO pilots.

The humanitarian role Canada's troops play is similarly hurt. Our lack of readiness is partly to blame for the delay in evacuating Canadians from Sudan in 2023 and for our inability to provide the Disaster Assistance Response Team to help Türkiye following the earthquake that same year. In Haiti, gang wars took centre stage after the president was murdered. Although Canada has the largest Haitian diaspora of any country (concentrated in Quebec), our reduced military capabilities did not allow us to play a direct role. To assist Haiti with its recent turmoil, two small Canadian vessels patrolling the Mediterranean off the coast of North Africa had to be rerouted to the Caribbean after the PM committed to doing something about the crisis while at a Three Amigos summit. At the time of writing, Canada is sending a group of seventy military trainers to Jamaica to train Haitian police in dealing with gang warfare.

To implement the government's new Indo-Pacific strategy in light of the threat posed by China, all the CAF could manage was to reroute a single ship from the Atlantic to the Pacific. As one of Canada's greatest historians, Jack Granatstein, has said, "Beijing must be shaking in its boots." The Commander of the RCN has repeatedly stated that this commitment will be hard, if not impossible, to maintain. At our strongest, we had three ships out for a few months, but they had to return to Canada and we could not sustain the mission.

* * *

THE MILITARY

How long the CAF can continue to perform their assigned missions through rotations, replacements, and resupply is a critical issue. It speaks to the availability of replacements—trained units, individual personnel and equipment, as well as the availability of supplies.

In operations, those supplies include ammunition, rations, and spare parts. Vehicles and equipment break down or are destroyed or damaged and must be repaired or replaced. Military personnel can serve for some time but need to be rotated out to rest and recover, and casualties must be replaced. In WW2 operations, units would stay in action until they were attritted to a point where they were ineffective (about 15 percent losses, as mentioned before) and then would be taken off the line.

Sustainability really means the ability to maintain forces in operations. In NATO circles, land forces must be able to deploy with three days' worth of supplies and a complement of thirty days' reserve of, among other things, ammunition, spare parts, and rations. Logisticians and support personnel are experts in determining the required supplies, but the fog of war means it's an inexact science. We have read reports, for instance, of the Ukrainian army using much more artillery ammunition than was originally planned. Calculations may be correct, but war is unpredictable.

Reports indicate the CAF are now at a very low supply of ammunition, drained by our commitments to Ukraine and the government's inability to support our industry so it could rapidly replenish the stocks. In wartime, Canada's industry ramped up very quickly and was able to effectively produce supplies and replacement equipment, but during this relatively peaceful time, the military supply industry has been left to wither on the vine. Again, building up Canada's supplies of ammunition, spare parts, and rations should be part of a national defence and industrial strategy.

The RCN does not have enough ships to protect our littoral territory or to sustain government strategies like the aforementioned Indo-Pacific plan. Worse, there are not enough crews to man the ships we do have. During the Afghanistan conflict, Canada lost a huge number of vehicles to enemy activity, especially IEDs. Our RCAF is missing a great number of pilots so that the few aircraft we do have in the inventory cannot be flown.

* * *

As mentioned above, it has been widely reported that the CAF are short of as many as 16,500 military personnel. The crisis in recruitment has many causes. The military, which is based entirely on rank and relies on obedience to orders to operate, has been revealed to have its share of predators. In response, the Department of National Defence has been working to root out individuals who have perpetrated misconduct of any kind, especially sexual misconduct, and prosecute them to the full extent of the law. In addition, the Canadian Forces are attempting to create a culture that maintains the discipline required to operate but ensures the safety and security of all its members. These actions are necessary and perhaps long overdue, but the fallout from the misconduct allegations and the portrayal of the forces as misogynistic and unwilling to change have certainly impacted recruiting.

The West's recent obsession with gender and identity issues, the CAF's relaxation of dress codes and focus on personal expression in an attempt to appeal to special-interest groups has not helped boost recruiting numbers. We seem to push to include those who do not necessarily want to join, thus alienating, and sometimes even frightening the demographic who have traditionally wanted to wear the uniform and serve. It is time to reinstate simple and inclusive meritocracy into the recruiting process and to integrate cultural changes into regular business processes. Personnel costs account for about half the total military expenditures; they need to be stabilized and restricted positions filled.

The apathy of our successive governments towards the CAF also does not help recruiting. Our decades-old equipment, lack of participation in operations around the world, and constant need to make do with meagre resources will never draw in talented recruits. Existentially, the notion of post-nationalism has removed Canadian heroes from our landscape, impairing the belief that service to our country is an honourable and appealing career. The militaries of other nations are facing similar difficulties in recruiting. The US, as usual, appeals to patriotism, but the strategy has had little impact on those from Generation Z they are trying to recruit. That is an ominous truth: if the current generation does not serve in our military, who will?

In Canada, our recruiting efforts aimed at under-represented groups have not been as successful as some would like. We could ask, "who will fight for Canada?" Here again, inclusive meritocracy should be the norm; we should encourage all who want to serve, including the groups we are targeting, focus on getting the best candidates, and not penalize those who are NOT from under-represented groups. Perhaps our effort to remove CAF bases from urban centres has also hurt our ability to recruit from under-represented groups. In essence, you have to fish where the fish are.

The focus on culture change has not had a positive impact on recruiting. For the last five years, the CAF has placed so-called inclusivity issues above operational capability. The forces have worked hard to change their culture, creating a new group subordinate only to the chief of defence staff to deal with these issues. I believe it is time now to accept the findings, applaud the changes that made the CAF a better place to be, and admit that some other policies—for instance, allowing man-buns, nail polish, and facial tattoos—have had no positive impact on recruiting and move on. A walk-back of the relaxed dress and grooming regulations is apparently in the offing at time of writing. Safe and secure reporting chains have been established for everyone, the class action lawsuit payouts are ongoing, and the dress regulations are being amended; it is time to roll all these efforts into the regular business of the military and return to prioritizing operational success.

There are some who want our CAF to drop the "warrior culture," including conformity and uniformity, because they feel these are the wrong paradigms for an effective and operationally ready military force. This is unwise. We have done away with the harassment and abuse of the past, which was to some extent rooted in that culture, and our cadre of instructors and non-commissioned officers know exactly how to make an effective fighting force—I have total faith in these individuals. If our military's most demanding fighting operations do not demand warriors with emotional fortitude and resilience, what do they require? Let's not put weak individuals in positions that demand mental strength and fighting abilities; that is what an operational military requires.

* * *

There are real experts who can speak about the issues surrounding the Canadian military procurement processes. I am not one of them. I have seen the process work on occasion to provide good, useful equipment in the appropriate amount of time. One example is the acquisition of the CF-18 fighter plane. The requirement to purchase new fighter aircraft was initially identified in 1977; the decision to procure the CF-18 was made in 1980; and the first aircraft was delivered in 1982, a mere five years later, thanks in large part to a future chief of defence staff, General Paul Manson. Five years from requirement to fielding the CF-18 forty years ago!

Fast-forward to the present: Canada's 2017 Defence Policy notes that "70 percent of all projects have not been delivered on time." Why? Without being glib, the first issue might be political meddling which results in an acquisition process that can be decades long. A few examples: when Canada was involved in Afghanistan, procurement decisions were being made relatively quickly and equipment was coming online in good time. The procurement process has an accelerated option called Urgent Operational Requirement (UOR), and this process was used regularly during our involvement in Asia. Some will remember our troops deployed to that desert-and-mountain environment with the green camouflage pattern combat uniforms made for a war in Europe. No one had anticipated that Canada would ever be fighting in a conflict area as arid as Afghanistan. So, a UOR was quickly developed allowing our troops to receive desert camouflage and better blend into the terrain of the battlefield.

We had decided that the tank was no longer a weapon of choice on a new battlefield dominated by long range missiles, artillery, lighter vehicle use, and asymmetric warfare. We had begun to dispose of our inventory. But as we faced organized Taliban units, it was realized, again, that the tank is the best protected direct-fire weapon out there. So, we urgently approached our allies and managed to lease tanks from Germany until we could purchase our own from the Dutch. Naturally, there will be some who continue to announce the death of the tank as a weapon system, especially considering the losses suffered in Ukraine, many to cheap drones. But tanks will remain a vital piece of the inventory, understanding that they need to be employed as part of an all-arms team.

We had neglected to procure our own strategic transport aircraft, preferring to lease heavy air transport when we needed it. Afghanistan demonstrated that leasing assets only worked outside an emergency, so a decision was made quickly to buy American C-17s. Amazingly, these aircraft were delivered over only a few months, showing that with a quick political decision and will, material can be procured rapidly.

I don't believe such a procurement success could happen today. The process is beset with gatekeepers that seem to slow down every step needed for success. There is regular political meddling: each contract must include industrial benefits that match the total cost of the procurement. There are many government departments involved, sometimes competing instead of collaborating with each other, and some of the employees in these departments are not always trained and experienced in procurement or are not available. Many of the missing military personnel are procurement staff who would be managing procurement projects. It also seems to me that Canadians can never buy equipment off the shelf; when they do, they insist on Canadianizing every little bit of the kit possible, adding millions of dollars to the cost. The ability for Canadian industry to build equipment in our yards is also limited in scope and size.

One of my colleagues, Ian Mack, a retired admiral and former procurement executive with the Department of National Defence, said in a report in early 2024, "timely delivery in the exceptionally uncertain and risky business of complex acquisitions is anything but common, even when experienced clients enable competent prime contractors by establishing project requirements and performance parameters." We need to fix this issue; doing so will save Canadians dollars, but more importantly it will deliver the operational equipment our military needs on time to be effective and save lives.

* * *

In many militaries, the permanent or regular full-time forces are backed up by a larger proportion of part-time forces that can undertake temporary missions as required or reinforce the regulars. In Canada, the numbers are reversed. The permanent military has been structured with some 70,000 regular-force sailors, soldiers, air personnel, and special force members, while the reserves usually number between 25,000 and 30,000.

To get a sense of the Canadian reserves, understand that they volunteer to don the uniform and serve part time, without legislative protection of their civilian jobs, so usually on their own holidays or in their free time. They are paid for the hours they work; they must meet the same training standards as full-time (regular) military personnel; and they may volunteer for full-time employment, such as on international missions. In the two world wars and Korea, our small regular, permanent cadre of service personnel were not those who primarily fought and won the victories for our country. Those who enrolled, were trained, and then jumped into the crucible of war were ordinary Canadian volunteers not unlike the reservists of today—workers from every job and region of our country.

Today, our tiny regular forces would likely assume a similar training role for mobilized reservists in a major conflict.

Unfortunately, the reserves have always been the runt of the litter of the forces, with a budget easy to cut when pressure for cuts is applied. An army reserve unit, for example, is given a budget that is calculated on the members training thirty-seven days a year. However, mandated training sessions, such as information security, ethics, gender-based assessment, the use of fire-fighting equipment, take more than twelve days off that total, leaving less than twenty-five days for actual military training. In addition, because of a lack of full-time personnel support in the reserve units, some of that training time is spent on administration, paperwork, and form-filling. Reserve budgets have never been fenced, so they could always be raided by the regular force.

The result is the less the budget, the less training days a commanding officer (CO) can schedule for his or her subordinates: fewer sailing days, less time on the ranges, fewer flying hours. Recently, a departmental report stated that some 50 percent of all defence equipment is unserviceable; but in the reserves, the situation is even more dire—no equipment, no training, but more sweeping of the hangar floor. Then there are ammunition allotments: some reserve artillery units today are only allotted ammunition to fire blank rounds for ceremonial events—there are no live rounds for real training. Sailing, training, and flying are what motivate young men and women to join, so cutting those activities has a huge detrimental effect on recruiting. The relaxation of personal grooming regulations has also not improved recruiting though the rules may be changing.

There are benefits to strong reserves beyond supporting the regular force. One is the footprint they provide for the armed forces across the country. In small rural communities, the reserves are usually the only contact citizens have with the military.

The reserves count against the portion of the federal budget devoted to the CAF, so increasing the reserves and making them more operational might be a good way to increase the percentage of Canada's GDP devoted to the military, as requested by NATO and pledged by successive prime ministers.

Let's say the government plans on increasing the size of the CAF to around 80,000, but then also increases the size of the reserves to 100,000. The resulting economic benefits would be huge: building armouries to house the reserve units and enhancing industrial capacity to produce equipment are just two examples of economic stimuli. The first mission of the regular forces would remain as first responders to operational missions in Canada and abroad, but their second most important priority would be to effectively support the reserves.

In my own time in the service, I was never posted to a regular support position with the reserves. But while commanding first my squadron and then my regiment, I made it a priority to improve our relationship with the reserves in my area. As a major and squadron commander, I developed a close relationship with my opposite number, Major Michel Grondin, and I ensured my officers got to know Michel's subordinates. Michel and I had been lieutenants and joined around the same time, me with the regular force and him with the Militia 12e RBC. Our regiment supported our Militia counterparts through training and mentoring.

As my career continued, I thought more regular-reserve collaboration would be beneficial. Before my appointment as the commanding officer of 12e Régiment blindé du Canada in Valcartier in 1989, I decided I would continue these efforts. One of my first actions as CO was to call together the COs of all four reserve armoured regiments in Quebec to pledge my support while I was at the helm. One of my predecessors had put in place a system where most of the vehicles used for training by the reserves would be housed and maintained in our garrison. We looked after all the Cougars that belonged to the Quebec armour reserve regiments—12eRBC(M) in Trois-Rivières, Sherbrooke Hussars, Royal Canadian Hussars in Montréal, and Régiment de Hull in Gatineau. This enabled the reservists to spend more time training on weekends, as they just showed up at the regiment and could then drive straight to the training area of Valcartier without wasting time on administrative or maintenance issues. One Cougar was usually left at each armoury so static training could take place. I thought this was a brilliant way to support the militia. At the same time, my regiment had the benefit of being able to use the equipment outside of the reserve training periods.

This regular-reserve collaboration culminated in my training and deployment of an entire squadron of reservists on our mission to Cyprus in 1990–91 for a six-month operational tour. I had made up my mind early that I was going to bring a militia squadron as part of my unit. So, I asked each of the four militia regiments to provide me with a troop (platoon). My only stipulation was that I would put 10 percent regular personnel in the squadron to set them up for success. One regiment, the Sherbrooke Hussars, provided me with a major to command the squadron, Major Dan Braun. I assigned him a second-in-command from the regular force, a regular-force sergeant-major and a regular-force quartermaster. Each troop had a lieutenant from the reserves, and I gave each a warrant officer second-in-command. Other regular-force personnel were placed in the squadron up to the level of 10 percent. The esprit-de-corps in each troop from the four regiments was outstanding.

The squadron came to train with us before we deployed, and I used them in exactly the same manner as the regulars once we were in theatre. The experiment worked beautifully, and I had as much faith in that squadron as in the regular force squadron; they were just as effective. On my return in April 1990, the commander of the army, at that time Lieutenant-General Kent Foster, asked to be briefed on the project. I spoke highly of the militia and what they could accomplish given the proper support. I'm not sure anything came of it, but in my anecdotal discussions since with different militiamen, they have told me that whenever they were involved in a 10/90 effort, they were successful.

In the army, your regimental affiliation and loyalty is extremely important. In 1994, as a colonel, I was appointed director of the Royal Canadian Armoured Corps. I made the decision (not very popular) to have all the armour regular support staff (RSS) re-badge to the regiment they were supporting instead of retaining their regular unit affiliation. I thought this would enhance the loyalty of the regulars to their militia unit. In fact, my vision was that these personnel would only remove the reserve regiment badge if they were posted back to another unit; if they went to a headquarters after their time as RSS, they would retain the militia badge. Eventually, it would be impossible to tell if a soldier or officer was a full-timer or part-timer; in my simple mind, it was a great way to support our reserves and reduce the void between the reserve and regular components of the army.

I have always thought that the regular force's first mission is operations and its second is support to the reserves; in that vein, had I commanded the army, my first act would have been to put 10 percent regular personnel in every reserve unit. This would enable the reservists to use all their time to train instead of doing paperwork, maintenance, etc. Many reservists transfer to the regular force once they get a taste of operations; transfer in the opposite direction is much more difficult. There must be a way to facilitate the transfer from the regular to the reserve forces, thereby providing experienced personnel to reserve units who can reinforce training and operations. On the other hand, I was saddened to learn that the reserve budget is often pilfered by the regular force. The army went through some bad times, and is still going through them as a result of our government not funding the CAF adequately, but we should endeavour to protect the militia budget. After all, the militia won our wars, not the regulars.

Closer cooperation between the reserves and regular force would yield immediate improvement in both their capability and their capacity to support operational missions. Domestic operations could be immediately undertaken by a larger reserve; for example, in floods and wildfires that go beyond the capabilities of civilian responders, the reserves would be deployable and effective. The reserves could and should be a national institution where both new and old-stock Canadians serve together, learning about the country, about our values, and about each other. Benefits such as fast-tracked citizenship could be offered to those who would undertake service in the reserves, just as they could be offered to regular-force recruits.

* * *

The issues listed above are not the only ones afflicting the CAF. But all of these and more are indeed having an impact on the serving personnel. Some serving commanders I have heard from report that units have lost more qualified operators in the last twelve months than in the last twelve years. These leaders are forced to triage missions in order to maintain a minimal ability to operate. A young leader wrote me the "principal concerns of the personnel are the mission (as always), to get the equipment needed to do the job, and the challenge of pursuing a leadership role in a difficult financial context with a directionless and politicized cadre."

The Conference of Defence Associations (CDA) Institute published an open letter in 2023 from sixty-two prominent Canadians decrying the dreadful state of our CAF and calling for immediate action by the government to rectify decades of neglect. I found it interesting that many of the issues raised in the letter were prominent in my Vimy Award acceptance speech from the year before. However, I was not invited to sign. The letter specifically called out the government's failure to give higher priority to Canada's defence, to redress the woeful state of the CAF, and to meet its commitments to allies.

The first issue to redress is the attitude of the government, and of Canadians, to national defence. It must be seen as important, not just on Remembrance Day, but throughout the year. This attitude correction should be guided by a comprehensive strategy, led by the prime minister and all of government that highlights the essential nature of defence, the honour of service, and the benefits of security and sovereignty. During our busy operational peacekeeping and Afghanistan missions, the term "whole-of-government" was often used to describe a pan-government effort to support a particular mission. In the effort to redress the issues facing the CAF, such an effort is exactly what is required. In the face of the global security situation, some nations are re-instituting some sort of national service. As a start, a whole-of-government discussion on a Canadian version of such service would be appropriate.

Second, these deficiencies are a result of the meagre funding accorded the CAF. As previously mentioned, NATO political leaders, including Canada's, agreed to spend 2 percent of their country's GDP on defence as a minimum but we have never achieved it. A bigger problem is the constant instability of what is spent on defence, meagre as it is. As one of the few discretionary budgets in the government program, it is easy to cut when trying to reduce overall spending. The announcement in 2023 that defence will be cut by nearly a billion dollars over the next three years is emblematic, and notwithstanding the minister of defence's preposterous statement that "there are savings to be had," more cuts will worsen readiness and capability.

Looking at the current annual deficits and the huge debt Canada is carrying, no government will likely have the will or ability to meet the 2 percent target in the next few years. The government nevertheless needs a plan. A prudent and common-sense approach might be to commit to raising the current defence budget, which sits at some 1.3 percent of GDP, by a certain amount (say 0.1 percent) every year and to protect the budget by making it non-discretionary and stable. All government departments would need to be involved in this effort as defence should not have to compete for funds.

With stable and steadily increasing protected funding, recruiting goals might have more of a chance to be met and the personnel situation redressed. The different CAF schools could be fully manned. The reserves could be reinforced as an insurance policy. Equipment purchases could be planned over time with less chance of being de-scoped or delayed because of unplanned budget cuts. Training expenses are one of the frequent casualties of budget cuts that impact readiness; with stable funding, training could be planned and conducted over the long term, and participation in international exercises could resume, thereby increasing readiness and interoperability. Sustainability would increase with well-trained and equipped units ready to replace those on current missions.

The April 2024 defence policy update focussed on the north, a direction I fully support for our forces. Let's imagine the good we can do if we are able to assume complete responsibility for the defence of the northern reaches of our continent; it is our backyard, after all. This should be a focus for our military; as a northern nation with a hardy people and with the help of our First Nations, we could become the protectors of *North* America. It can be a great focus for the CAF: northern basing for aircraft and land forces; increased sovereignty operations; increased patrolling by the RCN using new ice-capable ships and nuclear-powered submarines; increased collaboration and leadership among our northern peers, especially NATO partners such as Norway, Sweden, and Finland; and increased deterrence of possible enemies and environmental terrorists. Such an approach could be part of a national security strategy that would be developed by a thinking and common-sense government with a vision for our country and for Canadians. Of course, the huge distances in northern Canada are a real challenge to any surveillance or operation effort. However, there are many innovative ideas that can help in this regard. The use of airships is one recent approach that is being explored. They could be used for cargo replenishment of military and civilian communities and provide persistent surveillance over a wide area. We must attempt to leverage any good ideas that emerge from Canadian and international innovation.

As an armour officer, I understand the need for strong logistics in any operation, even if it is not sexy: bullets, fuel, food, and maintenance. Currently, the CAF ammunition reserves have been depleted below our own requirements and below our NATO commitments. The relationship between industry and the CAF is such that ramping up the production of ammunition will take months. The Canadian government can do a much better job of ensuring that the military-industrial complex in Canada is able to produce the required stocks of ammunition, rations, and other requirements for future and current operations. A military-industrial strategy is required identifying timelines, suppliers, and funding.

The defence policy update pledges to improve the production of ammunition stocks, in particular artillery ammunition. The Russia–Ukraine war has shown that the use of artillery ammunition is much greater than originally thought. Canada's reserve ammo stocks are woefully low and need to be restored. Production capability must be protected and able to ramp up quickly.

The chief of defence staff announced his retirement in the summer of 2024. Whoever will succeed him must not minimize the issues of readiness and sustainability of the CAF. As the commander of all military forces in Canada and the military advisor to government, the CDS must have a voice and must exercise it loudly—even if the minister of defence and the government are not happy to hear it—to ensure the security and defence of our country. Our forces need action to redress their obsolescence, and they need it now. Leaders at all levels must protect their subordinates from the inaction of others and this starts at the very top with the government. Our prime minister must be seized of the issue, he must infect his cabinet with the importance of the issue, and ministers must ensure the message is relayed within all departments.

Canada's role in the world and our international reputation have been shaken by the actions of our leaders and our disregard for our own security and sovereignty. Strong Canadian Armed Forces with high readiness and the ability to participate successfully in operations and exercises will ensure our country is secure and sovereign and able to defend itself against any aggressor. It will also demonstrate to our allies that Canada is no longer a free rider.

CHAPTER 10

Veterans

AS EXPLAINED PREVIOUSLY, SERVING in our armed forces means you accept the moral contract between yourself and Canadians. A contract implies two parties who come together to agree to trade something for something else. In the case of the moral contract between Canadians and their armed forces, each side commits to something.

On one side, members of the CAF commit to serve the country to the best of their ability, and to fulfil every mission they are asked to perform. At the top end of these potential missions is war. They agree to fight for Canada if required and if asked by their country, with all that this implies. The ultimate liability clause is the one distinguishing feature that separates the military profession from all other professions: service to country may cause you to die or to order others to put their lives in danger. This is one side of the moral contract.

On the other side, Canadians agree to do their part in exchange for this pledge of ultimate liability: to provide the military with everything they require to be successful in their mission—equipment, training, education, leadership, and support. This support *must* include looking after them once they hang up the uniform or return from duty. Let's look at the status of this moral contract today, specifically as it applies to veterans. I believe it, too, is broken.

The Department of Veterans Affairs was created in 1944. As a rule, it is staffed by career civil servants, some of whom have never met a veteran. But any veteran can tell you stories of the hoops they have to jump through to get basic medical care or the callous way their concerns have been treated. You might think I am exaggerating—I am not. This actually happened: a veteran asked for a wheelchair ramp for his home; in lieu of this, he was sent pamphlets on medically assisted suicide.

Prime Minister Trudeau promised during his 2015 election campaign that veterans would not have to fight the government in court for support and benefits. After two years of fighting the government in court, Brock Blaszczyk, a veteran who lost a leg to an IED in Afghanistan, reminded the prime minister of his promise at an Edmonton town hall meeting in 2018. "I was prepared to be killed in action," Blaszczyk said. "What I wasn't prepared for, Mr. Prime Minister, is Canada turning its back on me." The reply this young veteran received from the prime minister should have made Canada weep: "Why are we still fighting against certain veterans' groups in court?" responded the PM, "Because they are asking for more than we are able to give right now."

It is telling that this exchange took place six months after the government issued a formal apology along with a $10.5 million cheque to Omar Khadr, a convicted Al Qaeda terrorist (US Military Commission Court of Law) who in the summer of 2002 killed an American medic, Sgt Christopher Speer, with a hand grenade during a firefight in Afghanistan. The apology and the deal were kept secret from the Canadian public until presented as a fait accompli.

An inquiry in early 2024 reported that Nova Scotia veteran Lionel Desmond, who killed his wife, his daughter, his mother, and then himself in 2017, suffered from severe post-traumatic stress disorder (PTSD). He had been forced to deal with issues of treatment continuity: it took four months to get follow-up treatment after his release from a stabilization residential program. The report made twenty-five recommendations aimed at improving support for veterans and their families.

These actions, and inactions, by the government make it abundantly clear that veterans in general are very low on its list of priorities. This should anger all Canadians, not just those who wear, or once wore, the uniform.

* * *

Another example of veterans having to fight their government to receive support involves WW2 and Korea veterans.

Canada's role as one of the Allies during WW2 is well known. At the end of the conflict, our country of 11 million had contributed more than a million sailors, soldiers, and air personnel to defend our freedom. Some statistics: 45,000 Canadians were killed; 54,000 were wounded, 29,000 of them requiring long-term care. From 1950 to 1953, during the UN operation in Korea, 26,000 Canadians served, 516 died, and more than 1,000 were wounded. These heroic men and women have since, and always will be known as the "greatest generation."

As our fighters returned from these conflicts, the Canadian government built or acquired hospitals across the country to house the wounded and sick. Later, as health care became increasingly a provincial responsibility, Veterans Affairs Canada began transferring these hospitals to the provinces and provided a monetary allowance to maintain a higher level of care for each veteran housed in the hospitals.

In 2016, only one hospital remained to be transferred, Ste. Anne's Hospital (SAH) in Montréal. At the time, this 450-bed hospital still housed more than 300 veterans of WW2 and Korea. The average age of the veterans was ninety-two. The services and care these veterans received from VAC personnel were second to none and included bilingual staff, efficient and caring nurses and personal support workers, and on-site medical services 24/7. Personnel turnover was rare, and most had served at the hospital for many years. They and the veterans had become family. Because of their advancing age, the hospital was losing one or two veterans per week and incoming admissions were not enough to fill the empty beds. The province of Quebec was, therefore, anxious to take over the hospital and its empty beds for its own elderly civilian population.

After more than ten years of negotiations, the two levels of government agreed to transfer the hospital on April 1, 2016. A transfer agreement was signed which included the creation of a Transition Committee to oversee the transfer for three years. This committee would be composed of representatives of the governments of Canada and Quebec, SAH and the West Island Health Centre leadership, and one representative of the veterans. I was appointed by the deputy minister of Veterans' Affairs and my old friend General (retired) Walter Natynczyk, to the transition committee as the representative of the veterans housed at the hospital.

During the negotiations, the parties had agreed to ensure the continuity of care for the veterans that existed before the transfer. The ministers had also promised publicly and privately to veterans that the level of services and care provided to veterans would not be reduced.

Inexplicably, the transition committee met for the first time several months *after* April 1, after the hospital had been transferred. Therefore, there was no opportunity to review the transition plan, to ask questions, or, most importantly, to ensure the departure of personnel would be mitigated to maintain the level of service provided. Incredibly, and without the transition committee having been able to influence the decision, 40 percent of the staff departed with retirement packages on the day of the handover. The others agreed to remain under provincial management at the hospital.

From that time, the hospital was unable to recruit sufficient staff to provide the agreed level of services. The management hired temporary agency personnel whose training was woefully inadequate; most did not know what a veteran is, and many were unable to speak English (half the veterans were English-speaking) and often did not understand what these men and women had sacrificed for Canada. A mere few weeks after the transfer, in the middle of this chaos, the West Island Health Centre forced the hospital to admit a large number of civilian patients from the region who had experienced a loss of autonomy. This put additional pressure on the already overworked, undertrained, and undermanned staff.

This combination of factors had an enormous impact on the quality and level of care received by veterans. The impact was felt in many ways: long wait times for meals, ablutions, or baths; long wait times for diaper and urine bag changes; poor and often late response to emergencies; mistakes in medication; negative attitude of personnel; inability to communicate; and long wait times for specialist medical support (now only available outside SAH). Evenings and weekends were especially difficult for veterans.

Dealing with the fait accompli of the transfer, the transition committee was never able to remedy the situation and the veterans suffered greatly. Although I asked several times for statistics comparing monthly deaths before and after the transfer, I received nothing. It is possible to speculate that deaths increased when the veterans' routine changed and they lost their usual caretakers; several nurses with whom I spoke confidentially are convinced that the reduction in care from the loss of personnel actually resulted in the death of a number of veterans.

Several solutions were proposed to both levels of government and the regional authorities to alleviate the situation. For example, I proposed that a special team from VAC or the province could reinforce the hospital until the staff situation could stabilize. I also proposed slowing the transfer of civilian patients into SAH until sufficient staff was hired. These solutions were deemed too difficult.

To provide an idea of the impact of the transfer on veterans, 305 of them lived at SAH on April 1, 2016. At the end of September 2018, there were only 166 veterans left in residence. Their age on average was 95, with 6 over 100. As of today, fewer than 50 remain.

Unsurprisingly for this greatest generation, the veterans themselves acted. In February 2019, the Quebec Superior Court authorised a class action lawsuit by one of the residents, my friend Lieutenant Wolf William Solkin, on behalf of all those having lived in SAH or their surviving families. Lieutenant Solkin was the most vocal of the veterans decrying the reduction in care standards. This courageous man, prisoner of his adapted wheelchair or hospital bed, was still in full possession of his faculties at age ninety-four. With his iPad, he kept everyone informed of the situation (including ministers and the prime minister) and provided details of daily incidents. He had a network of dozens of employees who would confide in him as they witnessed the negative impact of the transfer on veterans and their services. Wolf became their voice and that of many veterans unable or unwilling to speak out. He managed to convince an intimidating team of lawyers to take on the class action.

The suit against the governments of Quebec and Canada and the West Island Health Centre aimed to demonstrate that the reduction in care and services for veterans was a breach of contract of the promises made to them. The class action also requested that the matter be dealt with swiftly, given the advanced age of the veterans.

Solkin's perseverance ultimately led to an out-of-court settlement. He signed the agreement on behalf of the members of the lawsuit two days before he passed away. The three defending parties agreed to pay a total of $19 million to all veterans who lived at SAH between April 1, 2016, and October 31, 2020, or to their heirs. Lieutenant Wolf Solkin had won his last battle for his fellow veterans. As he stated, "I believe that our government has failed to uphold its pledged commitment, has violated our right to health care as publicly promised, and has endangered our already fragile health and welfare, to the point of causing some premature deaths."

The fact is that these brothers and sisters in arms who sacrificed so much for us deserve not only our gratitude, but also the care, services, and attention they were promised. They deserve to live their last years comfortably and ultimately to die with dignity. The transfer of Ste. Anne's Hospital from federal to provincial authority robbed them of what they had earned. More appalling is that veterans had to sue their own governments to force them to uphold their end of the moral contract.

* * *

There are operational stress injury (OSI) clinics throughout Canada, some of which have been funded and run by VAC. These clinics treat military personnel and younger veterans suffering from PTSD on an outpatient basis. In regions where there is no VAC clinic close by, veterans are treated in the nearest civilian clinic. Ste. Anne's Hospital houses an OSI clinic, and it was part of my responsibility as representative of the veterans on the Transition Committee to ensure they would be looked after as the hospital moved from federal to provincial oversight.

SAH was special for two reasons. One, it was the only VAC clinic for OSI in Canada that included a residential section. In that facility of ten beds, veterans in crisis could stay for up to ninety days to recover and regain their stability; upon discharge, they would reintegrate into society and continue treatment as required on an outpatient basis. This residential clinic is where Lionel Desmond was stabilized before he returned to Nova Scotia and later killed his family. One of the issues raised in the inquiry report was that he had no treatment for four months after finishing the residential stabilization program.

Two, the facility was also multidisciplinary, with a pain clinic integrated within its structure. According to a VAC study, veterans suffer from chronic pain at twice the rate of Canadian citizens. Compounding that, 60 percent of veterans who suffer from an OSI also suffer from chronic pain and 60 percent of veterans who suffer from chronic pain also suffer from an OSI. Thus, the ability of veterans to be treated for chronic pain in the same clinic where they are treated for OSI is extremely beneficial.

Ste. Anne's Hospital, in short, was a wonderful place.

The residential clinic was exceptionally well set up and very private. It boasted individual well-appointed rooms, common areas and a kitchen, all clean and well-maintained. The Ste. Anne's Hospital Foundation (now the Quebec Veterans' Foundation) provided amenities over and above what the government was able to provide and was responsive to any missing or damaged furniture. The foundation also would obtain tickets to events in Montréal, such as hockey games or concerts, for the veterans to ensure they remained involved in society. Veterans at the residential clinic had immediate access to psychologists, psychiatrists, pain clinicians, social workers, orthopaedists, and other specialists who consulted with each other and closely followed each veteran. Nowhere else were the services as concentrated, and nowhere else could veterans be together with other veterans who understood each other.

I had several roundtable sessions with veterans housed within the residential clinic as well as other outpatient veterans with OSI issues to discuss their situation. They were, as veterans tend to be, *very* direct with me as I sought to find out where I could help. One of the side issues was the fact that yoga lessons were not approved by VAC as a therapeutic treatment for stress injuries whereas veterans kept telling me they received huge calming and stress-reducing benefits from these sessions. I was able to intercede, and yoga is now part of VAC-approved therapeutic treatment. SAH at one point wanted to condemn a side building where the yoga sessions were being conducted without providing a new locale; it eventually relented and found a room to accommodate veterans.

I handed over my role as a representative of the veterans in the summer of 2019. I had retired from the public service in 2018, and we had moved to the Niagara region, so I was no longer close to SAH. As well, the class action suit had been settled and my old friend Wolf had passed. In spite of this, I was keeping an eye on the situation there, and through my work with the Chronic Pain Centre of Excellence[2] in Hamilton, I was able to

---

2 The CPCoE was the first organisation to cancel me after my Vimy award speech in November 2022.

get regular updates. The biggest issue for the SAH residential clinic was, as it was for all our health services, the COVID-19 pandemic.

As a result of the pandemic and the close quarters within which veterans in the residential clinic lived, the clinic closed. Once the pandemic ended, the residential clinic did not re-open, and the staff reached out to me to see if I could apply any pressure. I wrote to the VAC staff I had come to know and asked questions. There are civilian residential clinics throughout Canada, but none are dedicated to veterans. I was sure that the issue was one of dollars, that VAC preferred to pay to outsource the service, and that VAC wanted to divest itself of the clinic and send veterans to civilian residential clinics. In my mind (and as I had discussed with many veterans), there was benefit in keeping veterans together in one location for companionship, camaraderie, and mutual support. It has been my experience that civilians do not easily understand and appreciate the challenges faced by service personnel, especially in difficult, traumatic situations—you just can't explain it properly. Only someone who has served can truly understand.

So, I advocated for the clinic to re-open, using a few ideas learned as a soldier, not as a doctor. In my reading of history, often the best way to treat shellshock in WW1 was to do so close to the front, where the soldiers could be with their comrades. Similarly, in WW2, many soldiers returning from the front did so on ships as a group, voyages that could last several days. The time allowed the men to discuss their experiences with each other, with their officers, with medical staff, and with clergy. Whether that counted as therapy, or perhaps simply closure, it seemed to help a great deal. It took us a little longer to grasp that during our mission in Afghanistan. Initially, we were getting soldiers home from the front as quickly as possible, proud to accomplish this feat in hours rather than days. The drawback of this approach became obvious very quickly. Many reservists were deployed during these missions, and they were attached to other units rather than serving with their own. Getting them home so quickly separated them from the unit with which they served in the mission; their comrades, friends, and everyone who truly knew what they had been through were now miles away. This resulted in feelings of isolation and abandonment. There was no one nearby with whom they could talk, share experiences or even tell tales over a beer. We learned quickly that this was not the ideal approach and soon had our soldiers spending a few days at an interim location to decompress and perhaps seek help before returning to their families. The benefit of keeping soldiers together where they could discuss their experiences, work through the trauma as a group, and have access to chaplains, psychologists, and social workers was immediately evident.

Despite the cost of keeping the residential clinic open, the benefits of creating such an environment for veterans in crisis are undeniable. I thought it was essential that VAC should re-open the residential OSI clinic. At the time of writing, it has not, and my sources state that there is no intention to do so.

* * *

My intent with this chapter was to illustrate a few issues that involve Veterans Affairs Canada and support to veterans in our country. There has been a proliferation of excellent associations and advocacy groups on social media that give advice to veterans and support them in their relations with VAC. Individuals I know, such as Bruce Henwood, Michael Blais and Guy Riel, also are making a difference in advocating for veterans and in effect forcing the government to look after them. The Royal Canadian Legion also does a lot to represent veterans, although younger veterans are at times reluctant to join. It is also sometimes difficult for all these organizations to speak with one voice.

These advocates are needed because, as I mentioned, VAC is a large bureaucracy with employees that have not necessarily served and may have little experience with veterans; they are just regular public service employees who get moved and posted like any others. I do feel it necessary to say that many VAC employees do care very much about veterans and try to help. Some succeed exceedingly well, and some are likely as frustrated as the veterans they serve. Perhaps the government could treat veterans as one of their favoured special-interest groups (God knows, it has many) and throw some money at their situations. Special training for all new and existing VAC employees would be an excellent place to start. Seeking to employ more veterans as staff of the department would ensure employees understand the situation. These approaches might also create areas for veterans to give back: they could create content for the training and deliver it. As veterans from a country that can afford it, they above all deserve support, and we should provide it.

CHAPTER 11

How to Move Forward

IN THE CHAPTERS ABOVE, I have written extensively on where I believe Canada has faltered, on the policies and ideals that have robbed Canada of its history, its values, its economic and military achievements, and that may harm its future if we stay the current course. I have also stated in no uncertain terms that I love Canada and I believe in Canadians and our potential to undo the damage, to embrace the tenets and beliefs that made Canada the great nation it was, and to make it so once again. Some of the chapters provided their own recommendations and reinforced the idea that Canada can recover. It is a tall order to be sure, but not impossible. In sum, I believe that effective leadership and service are what Canada needs to become great again.

* * *

The qualities that make a good leader have not changed and are more important today than ever. First, leaders *lead*. That is, they *accept* the mantle of leadership they have earned through their hard work, sometimes with a bit of luck. I am reminded of a story I once heard about one of our former chiefs of defence staff, General Jacques Dextraze, often called "Jadex."

A WW2 and Korea veteran, Jadex was the CDS when I joined the CAF in 1972 and I saw him once from afar as he landed in a helicopter on the RMC parade square for a visit. Even from a hundred metres away, I was filled with awe. I was watching one of my idols. Jadex had a reputation as a courageous hard-ass who had never aspired to the highest position in the CAF. The story goes that after his appointment was announced, he looked himself in the mirror and said something like, "You never asked for this appointment, and you never thought you would ever reach such a rank. But now you *are it*, and you are going to be the best you can be!" I must admit having had this type of conversation with myself when I became a general. In all cases, I tried to make sure I accepted the leadership responsibilities the military provides. A leader must not be reluctant but get on with the job.

In my military career and its aftermath, I was fortunate to meet and observe great leaders, to see them in action, to watch them handle the burden of leadership. I learned from them. I also encountered some poor leaders whose lessons were just as valuable. As a young officer, I kept a "leadership book," a simple notebook in which I jotted down notes on the experiences I observed or stories I heard. The idea was to write the date, context, and decisions made by the actors involved and determine whether the decisions made by that leader were successful. I still have my leadership book, and whenever I speak to aspiring leaders, putting together such a book is one of my recommendations. One of the ideas I used throughout my career was to "work for your successor." When I moved on, I tried to always leave the job better than I had found it. This might mean improving the processes, the accommodations, or the personnel. But in the CAF, when people are posted regularly in and out of jobs, that approach would ensure continuous improvement. Always work for your successor.

In conjunction with these real-life leadership notes, I developed my own set of leadership principles. When I was a young officer cadet undergoing armour training in CFB Gagetown, New Brunswick, there was a master warrant officer named Kenneth Maybee who took me aside and asked me what my principles of leadership were. Frankly, being a twenty-year-old at the time, I had never thought about it. So, I sat down and thought about what was important to me and how I would command or lead in my career. The four items mentioned earlier were the result of this contemplation. I have briefed every group I have since led so that they might understand me a bit better and understand what I deem important. I used these principles as a lieutenant with my first troop of sixteen soldiers all the way up to my multinational commands with NATO, OSCE, and the UN, and again as a civilian leader at RMC Saint-Jean with my professors and staff. In my estimation, the principles worked with all these groups and fit all these different contexts. I want to expand on them here.

Communications: Learn to communicate upwards, downwards, and sideways with everyone. Be aware, be prepared, speak the truth, even if you don't have all the answers. Talk to your subordinates, your peers, and your bosses; tell them what you are about. Tell them about your principles of leadership, what makes you tick, what pisses you off. Have an open-door policy: it may take a lot of your time, but the time you spend listening is well spent. Go see your people in their environment, ask them about their job, what they like and dislike. Seek those who do not think like you do, seek those who are considered a little off-the-wall, seek those who disagree with you and get their point of view. It will only make your plan better, even if it only confirms you made the right decision.

As I gained experience and progressed to higher ranks, I tried to make time and visit those doing the work. Sometimes, I learned more from direct discussions with subordinates than the information I received through the chain of command. As chief of staff of NATO SACT, I would speak directly to all members of the headquarters every three months; I would get all of them out on the lawn in front of the building and spend time giving them a sense of the work they had been doing. What we had gone through the last three months, what we could expect in the next three, and I would not let them go until I had been asked a few questions. That way, along with my walk-throughs at headquarters, they got some access directly to the COS. Always try to communicate directly.

Teamwork: Emphasize the importance of the team, united in the effort for the mission: no backstabbing, no tattletales, no cliques, no dividing. Cover for each other, be ready to help, be tolerant and open to other views. Help others to be better. And support your boss: he or she is your teammate, your battle buddy. Be prepared to sacrifice for the team. Teamwork also leads to resilience, something essential in trying times as you can then lean on each other.

Professionalism: Carry yourself as a professional and expect all others to do the same. This means treating everybody with respect, not tolerating any harassment, giving your all at work for the good of the service. Strive to progress, do better and keep learning. Come to work on time and give the King an honest day's work. Have principles and live by them. Behave as a professional whether anyone is watching or not. Also, dress with respect, whether in uniform or in civilian attire, and expect all others to do the same and be the example of that ethos.

Fun or Attitude: The only time you cannot have fun while in the army is when you are under direct attack. Our profession is fun, and leadership is fun. It is also an awesome responsibility—the military is allowed to legally carry weapons and to use them in the service of our country. It is a most rewarding profession, where we are charged with the security of the nation. In any context, a positive attitude is essential to your well-being and will be contagious for your colleagues. Compared to the vicissitudes suffered by our military predecessors, we have it pretty good. So have some fun, unless you are under artillery fire!

***

Former US secretary of state Henry Kissinger was interviewed by *The Economist* shortly before his death in 2023 at the age of 100. He warned the world of the importance of leadership to solve the ongoing issues that we are facing today. How true. When the world is in crisis, its citizens look to leaders. Sometimes these leaders rise to the top and provide us with solutions, hope, and comfort. Other times, they fail and prove themselves to be out of their depth. An effective peacetime leader, for instance, does not guarantee success in times of peril. I think we need look no further than our past to find examples of great leaders: Churchill and FDR of course, JFK and Reagan, Thatcher and Mulroney. And a military hero of mine who in post-war Japan proved that he was a great statesman, General Douglas MacArthur.

Each of these leaders faced difficult and complex issues and made courageous decisions; some may have been controversial at the time but have since been proven necessary. Today, President Volodymyr Zelenskyy of Ukraine has shown himself to be a tremendous leader. Personally brave, he has weathered Russia's unprovoked attack on his country and led his people's fight to defend their homeland. His nightly addresses are essential to the morale of his people, and his expertise at modern modes of communications, particularly social media, has kept the plight of Ukraine in the news and unforgotten, prompting allies to continue supporting the country.

All great leaders were and are great communicators. Communications are an essential part of leadership, and communication is not just speaking out. It also means listening; it is a two-way process. Communication is more critical than ever in this world of sound bites and mic dropping. A good leader ensures his followers know where they are going and how to get there. A great leader makes them want to go there. A great leader can take a seemingly insurmountable objective and make its achievement possible in the hearts and minds of their followers.

Communicating is also being precise in your ideas and your direction; here is an example of an imprecise mission that luckily did work. Once the Kosovo Verification Mission was evacuated from Kosovo by the chairman-in-office of the OSCE in March 1999, we found ourselves regrouped and awaiting next steps in North Macedonia, known in those days as the Former Yugoslav Republic of Macedonia (FYROM). My bosses at the KVM decided to organise a mission to support Albania as Milosevic was pushing Kosovars out of the country and flooding the border with refugees. As the poorest country in Europe, Albania was reeling under the pressure. So, I was tasked to head the KVM Refugee Task Force with the following very imprecise mission statement: "Go to Albania and see what you can do to help"! Though this mission statement was not what I was taught at CAF Staff College, it left me with latitude to observe where the government of Albania needed help and then to try to add value. I believe we did, to a great extent, but missions should be clearer.

Leaders must lead with courage. Sometimes decisions are difficult, and rarely does a policy please every constituent. It is up to the leader to sell it. There is a difference between deciding based on research and consultation and deciding because it is popular or it polls well. The best decisions are those made for the good of the whole, not just good for friends of the leader. If, in the long run, the decision is *truly* for the good of Canadians, it *can* be sold. A good leader must be able to explain the reasons behind the decision and have the courage to stand by it. Unfortunately, all too often today, special interests are the focus of leaders, trumping the collective good. Making decisions for the collective good requires strength of character, communications skills to explain to people, and a great deal of courage.

That quality—courage—remains one of the most important qualities in a leader. Courage of ideas. Courage in the face of criticism. Courage to guide and lead. Courage to create a vision for the good of all. Courage to sell that vision, to make even those who may not immediately benefit from it understand it is ultimately good for the whole and worth the sacrifice. Courage to recognize an error and to accept responsibility—personal responsibility—for that error. The concept of "falling on your sword" has gone out of favour in recent times. Publicly sporting a victim's cloak is far more coveted: "not my fault" is a common refrain, accompanied by a myriad of "others" upon which to place the blame. That can include society, parents, upbringing, colonization, generational trauma, intersectional trauma—the list is endless. Taking personal responsibility for our own actions has disappeared, but it must return, and it must become noble again. Apologizing on behalf of Canadians for supposed historical wrongs committed by Canada's forefathers is unfair to so many Canadians, including those who came as immigrants or are their descendants. It is also hugely unfair to make those apologies based on a judgment of history using today's standards.

Personal responsibility entails a duty of care for others: that requires us to find the elements that bind us as Canadians instead of looking for what divides us. And that's why one aspect of becoming Canadian, our citizenship ceremonies, is so important. If you don't believe that Canada is a nation, if your outlook has become post-national, you won't need citizenship ceremonies. A post-national state has no defining culture, so immigrants can just live as they did in their former countries and develop no allegiance or loyalty or patriotism towards Canada. In my view, this is the drawback of what we called the Canadian mosaic, where immigrants would form small enclaves of cultures separate from the whole. Today, I think we need to become more of a melting pot. But first we need to know what Canada is, what makes a Canadian, and what new Canadians are expected to sign up for. To do so, our leaders need to develop a vision for our country.

***

We often speak of how different we are from Americans. But what defines *us* as Canadians? To my mind, answering that is an aspirational objective. What does our country mean? What are its values? What do we *want* to be? Canadians need a grand vision to unite us, a vision that benefits the collective good and for which we are willing to make sacrifices. Our Fathers of Confederation were not perfect, but they created a prosperous and vibrant country, and did so without a bloody civil war. I believe the elements that made that achievement possible are values we should all endorse: common sense, freedom, security, hard work, personal and fiscal responsibility, family, tolerance, free markets, and a government that lives within its means.

Canada has produced great leaders in the past, among them John A. MacDonald, Wilfrid Laurier, and yes, Pierre Elliot Trudeau and perhaps Jack Layton, whose potential was left unrealized by his death. We are in desperate need of another great leader, one who will unite the country with a vision, provide common-sense solutions for our challenges, and most important, inspire all Canadians to love, be proud of, and contribute to this great country.

Some of Canada's past leaders had grand visions for our country, and most were worthy. Their success at achieving these visions is left for history to judge. Let's look at a few. *Canada and Speeches from the Throne*, a University of Regina textbook published in 2020, examines the prime ministers of the twentieth century. The Liberals had governed Canada for most of the twentieth century by the time John Diefenbaker's Progressive Conservatives were elected in 1957. During his tenure, he delivered seven speeches from the Throne and they "solidified his vision for One Canada, outlining the priorities of his Conservative Party to create a modern nation and prosperous future through membership in the Commonwealth, the development of the richness of Canada's resources, and the promotion of a united, un-hyphenated Citizenry." Diefenbaker wanted Canadians to be Canadians, not French-Canadians or English-Canadians, but simply Canadians. In a decade that saw significant European immigration, this was an important policy. "He believed in an inclusive Canada, recognized internationally as a champion for human rights." This vision is indeed worthy and many of its aims are as relevant today as they were in 1957.

Lester B. Pearson's speech from the Throne in 1967 celebrated Canada's centennial. Although admitting that the road to this anniversary had been bumpy at times, Pearson believed Canadians should be proud of how far they'd come. They should be proud of the nation created by the Fathers of Confederation. "The promise of a bright future for Canada came from its proud past." Pearson created two symbols of Canadian identity that demonstrated independence from our British rulers: the Canadian flag and the Order of Canada. Perhaps more important but less visible, his legacy will also be forever tied to peacekeeping, a practice he helped usher in globally and one that, as he saw it, demonstrated our ability to excel in an endeavour that distinguished us from Americans. He believed in the idea of a middle power, which Canada has proven to be, though that middle-ness was not without strength and influence. I feel this vision of Canada identifies and embraces the very real notion that although we can never be a global superpower, we could have a place on the world stage and a role that is important and fulfilling.

Pierre Trudeau delivered sixteen speeches from the Throne and came to power during a pivotal period of social change and unrest not just in Canada, but south of the border as well. At home, Quebec-Canada relations were deteriorating and a cultural pushback against the "old ways" was growing. Trudeau's policy of multiculturalism appealed to Canadians who were untrusting and frightened of the huge "melting pot" to the south. Halifax's Canadian Museum of Immigration at Pier 21 categorizes it as such: "Multiculturalism was intended to preserve the cultural freedom of all individuals and provide recognition of diverse ethnic groups to Canadian society." Its focus on diversity has been distorted and misused by practitioners of the radical social-justice ideology seizing the West at this moment.

Brian Mulroney, like Diefenbaker, was elected with a huge majority and his first speech from the Throne in 1984 described a new vision for Canada, "a new era of reconciliation, economic renewal, and social justice." He believed strongly that Canada had a rightful place in the world, and we could only achieve that through national unity. The Meech Lake Accord and the Charlottetown Accord both attempted to unify Canada, but both failed to be ratified by all provinces. Mulroney had more success internationally, culminating in the North American Free Trade Agreement. The pact highlighted a period in history in which Canada–US relations were at their most amiable.

Jean Chrétien came to power in 1994 with another Quebec sovereignty referendum on the horizon. He, too, emphasized national unity and included First Nations in that unity. He stressed economic stimulation and strong industrial production. At the end of his tenure in 2002, his final speech from the Throne spoke to Canadians about our involvement in the United Nations and other international alliances that showed Canada's commitment to world peace in the aftermath of 9/11. Climate change made its first appearance in his speech.

According to *Canada and Speeches from the Throne*, Stephen Harper "believed it was critical to restore government integrity as a virtue," and he was just as passionate about being tough on crime and restoring law and order to Canada's neighbourhoods. The financial crisis of 2008 shaped much of his economic policy, and he attacked what today we call gatekeepers in his efforts to streamline government efficiency. In my opinion, Harper's final speech from the throne was his very best:

> Consider this: we are honourable. People of peace, we use our military power sparingly; but when we do so we do so with full conviction, gathering our forces as men and women who believe that the freedoms we enjoy cannot be taken from us. This clarity focuses our might in terrible times. And wherever and whenever we unleash that might, we raise our grateful voices and our prayers to honour those who have stood in harm's way for us.

These past Canadian prime ministers had visions for Canada, visions that would empower and enhance the lives of our citizens. Most spoke of unity, many included pride in our military, in our past and most had a desire to see Canada contribute globally. Today, we need a new vision that will unite us and start the re-building process. We are divided, shaken, and weary of economic and social issues that have torn our national fabric to shreds. We need to be inspired to aspire to greatness.

Why does Canada not aspire to greater things? We desperately need leaders who can develop a vision for the entire country while respecting and embracing the differences of this vast land. This is not an easy task. In fact, I have often wondered whether Canada, with its geography and its myriad cultural differences, can be governed as one united country.

Canada is huge and its needs are just as large; its regions differ in many ways, and their preoccupations sometimes do not align. The Atlantic provinces, somewhat isolated geographically, depend on an economy at the mercy of the sea and the seasons. Maritimers are sometimes seen as the poorest Canadians and face economic hardship not seen in other parts of the country; they also have a tradition of serving in the military in greater numbers proportionally than other regions of Canada. Quebecers are obsessively proud of the fact that they are "distinct," and they are, but they insist on putting their language and culture above all others and always hang the threat of separation over the rest of Canada. This doesn't help to unite the country and has created an "us-vs-them" mentality. Ontarians do have a great opinion of themselves, and some believe they represent the real heart of Canada, with centre-of-the-universe Toronto as its unofficial capital. The incredibly resource-rich prairie provinces feel their economic potential is being choked by both climate activists and government gatekeepers. For decades, the rest of Canada benefitted from equalization payments from Alberta, but with serious internal and external pressures on the energy industry effectively shutting it down, the rest of Canada has been reluctant to step up for Alberta. British Columbia often seems a world of its own, more closely linked in its economy and political spirit to America's Pacific Coast than the rest of Canada. Our three northern territories are unique in extraordinary ways.

As noted in *Policy Options* in Sept 2022, "The territories represent unique case studies . . . due to vast geographies, dispersed populations, limited infrastructure and several other factors, providing services to northern residents is more expensive. These factors also inhibit higher levels of economic activity and resource development."

It will take a very strong leader to overcome these differences and deep-rooted resentments to push for one national vision. It's a challenge many of our leaders have proven unable to comprehend, let alone meet, but I have not given up hope.

***

In my view, we have lost the concept of big ideas and big national projects—ideas for the good of the entire country that fit within the vision for our country. The leaders who could develop and sell these to our citizens are few and far between. Collective good must again outweigh personal interests. Since Prime Minister Brian Mulroney—he was by no means perfect, though—there has been a lack of grand ideas, vision, and projects for our country. Mulroney brought us the goods and services tax (GST), NAFTA, and constitutional accords (yes, I know they failed but they were ambitious—the last honest efforts to sort out our constitution). Jean Chrétien and those who came after had no big ideas that could unite our country. Our leaders today seem to look at polls and then make small adjustments to improve their own electability. This is then touted as sound management.

Let me present a few big ideas that our leaders might consider:

Make Canada self-sufficient in energy by 2030: Natural gas pipelines and shipping terminals may not please the climate change alarmists in BC or the Quebec populace, but to the declining economies of our Atlantic provinces and the shrinking Alberta resource sector, they are a lifeline and must be supported. And if you think of the help our resources can provide for other nations, it is clearly the way we should be proceeding. At the same time, Canada should not depend on fossil fuels from illiberal nations who then profit from our dollars.

Improve Canada's military capabilities so we are able to defend ourselves and our values: Substantial increases in military funding are never attractive to Canadians obsessed with education and health care, but national security, sovereignty, and a voice in the future that echoes our own values is a message that can be understood by all Canadians if presented appropriately. Sovereignty and national security should be made a priority, at least in balance with competing social programs.

Complete a full free-trade agreement between provinces: Although 2017's Canadian Free Trade Agreement between provinces and territories has boosted commerce within Canada, there is still work to be done in order for competition to flourish between provinces and territories. Just as NAFTA and CUSMA (Canada–United States–Mexico Agreement) have helped our economy, true free trade between provinces would have a similar effect. DeLoitte estimates the economic benefit to be several billion dollars.

A Vision for Canada: Many large organizations and businesses work hard to develop vision statements. Such development is an effort that takes many hours of discussion focusing on core values, competencies, and shared interests. Everyone has a part to play in developing the vision so that everyone understands it, feels it is theirs, *adopts* it, and *works toward its success*. Once agreement is reached, every move by every employee or stakeholder must be made in accordance with the vision and must support the vision. The vision is aspirational and may not be what the organization is today, but what the organization will strive to be. A broad, non-partisan committee could develop a simple vision statement for Canada, perhaps starting with our constitution and other keynote documents that define our country. This statement could state the values our country represents.

The committee would include representatives from Parliament, the judiciary, First Nations, academia, the military, and general populace so that results could be presented to the House of Commons for approval, with the proviso that it would not be reversed by a change in government. The resulting grand national vision would be studied in schools, be part of citizenship ceremonies, and be a beacon of Canadianism to the world. All new immigrants to our country would learn it and understand what they are signing up for.

A Canadian Development Corridor: I must include what I consider a brilliant idea from one of Canada's heroes, RCAF Lieutenant-General Richard Rohmer, a WW2 RCAF veteran and Canadian hero, who just turned 100 at the time of writing. Rohmer is an accomplished (and Canada's oldest practicing) lawyer, an author, and a developer who also happened to fly 135 missions in P-51 Mustang fighters during WW2. He was most prescient in proposing what he terms a mid-Canada development corridor. Here is what he has in mind: the identification and development of a massive east-to-west belt of our country some hundreds of kilometres north of where most Canadians live, running from Labrador City, Newfoundland, through Flin Flon, Manitoba, to Fort Nelson British Columbia. This resource-rich corridor would follow the boreal forest and below the edge of the tundra, and contain new cross-country highways and railways and communications systems as well as new community developments to encourage citizens and new immigrants to move north. I say it was prescient because the idea was proposed around 1968. If climate change predictions come true, the earth will be warmer fifty years from now and the corridor will be temperate. It's not a crazy notion and other jurisdictions are taking the spirit of the concept seriously: the Ontario government is looking at developing the "Ring of Fire" and Quebec has proposed its "Plan Nord." Perhaps best of all, the plan would put our First Nations front and centre and would ensure their leadership and partnership in this initiative. *That* is a big idea.

Canadian international leadership as a middle power: The ideas above have been things Canada can do alone, but there are also things we can do in the broader world. I'd like to see us return to exerting leadership as a middle power. As both a middle power and a member of the G7, Canada can play an important role in the community of nations. The first requirement for Canada to regain its influence as a middle power is to settle on its identity, as mentioned above, and take principled positions that flow from that vision and its values with regard to the events of our times. How Canadians see themselves will affect how others perceive Canada. How others perceive Canada will reinforce our reputation and ability to influence other nations. As a middle power, Canada could, for example, propose that international humanitarian law and the laws of armed conflict be updated. The Geneva and Hague conventions were developed after WW2, based on the lessons learned in that conflict. They have not been significantly updated to take into account the new operational theatres, where terrorists, corruption and non-state actors in civilian clothes are the threat. From the huge death tool in Dresden and Hiroshima came the optimistic notion of proportionality of retaliation. In reality, it is singularly difficult to apply, but we expect it of the IDF in Gaza even though no country has worked harder to reduce collateral damage than Israel. What better country to lead this updating effort than Canada, who fought honourably and successfully in WW2, then was known as the world's peacekeeper, was a founder of the UN and NATO, and helped end apartheid in South Africa?

* * *

From our vision as a country, a national security strategy must flow, and then a defence strategy aligned with our national and global ambitions. The recent defence policy update has committed government to review the defence policy every four years. This is a good idea, but it must include more than just defence. Security in this uncertain world will entail not just military forces, but run the gamut of security aspects, including energy, industrial, and environmental security. We saw how big a role energy security has played in Europe since the beginning of Putin's "special military operation" in Ukraine. We must account for factors such as the protection of our natural resources, especially water. In my view, water will become as prized and as valuable as fossil fuels in decades to come. Canada currently has the third largest freshwater resources in the world after Russia and Brazil. We must establish a way to protect this resource while sharing it with those in need.

The prime minister should set up a national security council that he would chair with the appropriate ministers who have access to the levers of security. Our defence strategy would come next, distilling the elements of the security strategy that apply, commensurate with our level of ambition. Do we want to focus on the north? Do we want a blue-water navy that can reach out and touch the entire globe? Do we want an air force able to pull its weight in NORAD? Can our army protect Canada? Are our special forces able to fulfil their vital role? What role do we assign to our reserves?

Clear positions on these questions will enable all our leaders in Canada and our representatives abroad to understand the context and approach they should be taking. The French have a term called *la pensée du chef* that signifies a field commander explaining to subordinates what the overall aim of a mission is and the scheme of manoeuvre required to achieve the aim. In that way, if communication between the commander and subordinates is lost, the units will remember the commander's thoughts (his *pensée*) and continue in accordance with the aim. In Canada, we call it "mission command," but I think the French term is much more elegant. In any case, a clear vision and clear strategies will enable all to remain in *la pensée du chef*, the *chef* being Canada.

Next, Canada should assume a leading role in our alliances and with nations that share our values. Joining an alliance entails surrendering part of your sovereignty to that alliance; it is a huge commitment. However, the benefits lie with the common purpose and the collective strength of the whole. All nations would prefer to be able to defend themselves with their own independent means. But even the US, with its hyper-capable forces, prefers to fight alongside allies. Alliances bring strength from their diversity. While I was chief of staff in Norfolk, there were several times when innovative ideas and solutions to problems from smaller NATO nations were brought forward that surprised the more powerful members. I also thought that my headquarters, with some 600 personnel from navy, army, and air forces of (at that time) twenty-six nations, provided at least seventy-eight different ways of looking at the same problem to find a solution.

For Canada to count in and count on our alliances, we need to contribute to the UN, NATO, NORAD, and others with appropriate funding and meaningful positions. We need to pull our weight. Instead of virtue signalling and scolding others, we should focus on holding up our end of agreements. Leadership by example is needed. The CAF already benefit from many advantages compared to some nations' militaries. Most European militaries that joined NATO were steeped in Cold War thinking, anticipating defensive battles against the Warsaw Pact, fought on their own territories, without the need to be deployable over large distances. Within Canada, it is not possible to think of responding to a threat without having to deploy for hundreds, sometimes thousands of kilometres. So our forces have always been somewhat deployable in this manner; we don't need to overhaul our thinking. But today, with threats that are truly global in nature and our north coveted and vulnerable, perhaps an additional element of defence of our own territory needs to be explored.

* * *

Before ending this chapter, there are a few other elements of leadership worth mentioning. One is to resist the temptation to gain advantage by division. Today's leaders have a bad habit of rallying their supporters at the expense of their detractors. History has shown that success as a leader demands cohesion, unity, and respect of all those they lead, not just those who agree with them. How can this be achieved? A good first step is to look not at what divides us, but at what unites us: those values and strengths we all profit from, that make us who we are, that we should be proud of, that we should brag about, from coast to coast to coast. We must begin to see ourselves as part of a greater whole, to understand that a prosperous Alberta helps the rest of the country; that supporting the fisheries industry of the Maritimes makes all of Canada richer; joining Quebec in celebrating its European uniqueness encourages Quebecers to feel like they're part of Canada; that cherishing the vast and diverse North by ensuring its Canadians live well makes us all stronger.

Canada is a massive country with people from all walks of life, from every corner of the earth. It is not easy to unite us all for a single cause or to find a collective good. But imagine if pursuing that goal had been top of our leaders' minds in Ottawa in January 2022. Imagine if our prime minister had reached out to the Freedom Convoy immediately and acknowledged their right to protest, listened to their concerns, and opened a dialogue. Imagine how those following days might have turned out. I spoke earlier of the effort the PM made to speak with and listen to the Black Lives Matter protesters. I am outraged that he could not do the same with this other group of protesters.

Instead, even before they arrived in Ottawa, he dismissed the truckers and their supporters. He labelled them a "small fringe minority of people" with "unacceptable views." There was no room left for compromise, and the resulting chaos was not surprising. Instead of being an opportunity to unite, the events surrounding the Freedom Convoy will go down in history as some of the most divisive in Canadian history, potentially as damaging as the Quebec separatist movement and the current alienation of the Western provinces over resources. I cannot imagine a military leader or sports coach labelling half the team as deplorables or fringe radicals and then expecting them to fight, and win, as one. Today's leaders must find a way to unite, not divide. And that can only be done by listening and communicating respectfully with each other.

It is also important for leaders to recognize and support that easy-to-ignore segment of society, people who keep their heads down, work hard, and follow the rules; the "silent majority."

What happened to the idea that working hard is something to be proud of? Now it's seen all too often as something to be dodged and ridiculed. Learning the skills required and doing your job to the best of your ability with professional and ethical standards that have stood the test of time is still important. "Quiet quitting," not buying into the ethos of the company, doing the minimum requirements of the job and putting in no more time, effort, or initiative than absolutely necessary—these are the diseases in today's work force. Those who get away with it boast about it on social media; those who are caught sue their employers for wrongful dismissal or harassment. Yet hard work is needed now more than ever.

Canada was founded on the political principles of peace, order, and good government. Order, to me, also means rules and laws that protect our country and its citizens. You break the law, you suffer the consequences. Lawful peaceful protests are protected, but when they impact the economy such as the unlawful blocking of bridges or railways, the authorities need to have the courage to remove protesters—and not just those who clash with their political ideals. When protests at our universities foster anti-Semitism, the laws must be applied and the protesters removed forthwith. I believe our laws and regulations need to be upheld up and, yes, bail rules need to be tightened.

* * *

I think these same people who work hard and follow the rules tend to be patriotic Canadians. We need to do a better job of celebrating patriotism in Canada. We could begin by being prouder of the maple leaf that our soldiers wear on their uniforms and ensure no other flag take its place or flies above it. This is the flag that should fly front and centre on all our government buildings, the flag that can and should unite all Canadians. It stands for all our freedoms without regard to special interests, all equal under the law.

As I mentioned earlier, as a young officer, I had the honour of being trained by a superb individual who was black. Sgt Clayton taught me that one should respect the diversity of individuals be they black, white, Indigenous, or of a different sexual orientation. All of us served under the Canadian flag. He believed that this flag, the red maple leaf, represented all the diversity and inclusion that Canada embraced. This was a strong statement coming from a black man in the 1970s.

I love the Canadian flag. It represents everything I protected and worked for in my entire career in the service of our country. I also respect LGBTQ2+ people in our country, just as I respect Indigenous Canadians and those of colour. I understand the desire of Canadians to support Pride; my brother, Pierre, and his partner, Brian, have been together for more than forty-seven years and are part of the LGBTQ2+ community. I love them and respect them for being who they are and how they live. But there is only one flag that unites all Canadians, of any race, colour, religion, provenance, sexual orientation: it is the Canadian flag. It is not the Pride flag or any other special-interest group's flag. Any protocol expert will tell you nothing supersedes a nation's flag on its own territory.

Our flag is what our forefathers, our veterans, and our current serving military members fought to keep free in all the conflicts in which we have been involved. To this day, these men and women wear that flag on their uniforms while projecting our values across the world, despite the meagre resources our government provides them. We've all seen the American films where Old Glory was not to be dropped to the ground no matter if the bearer was shot. At some American universities, protesters in support of Palestine were tolerated until they tried to replace the US flag with that of Palestine. We are not Americans, and we sometimes roll our eyes at what we feel is their exaggerated patriotism, but in operations, in international competitions, our flag is what we play for. Our flag is what we show up for. Our flag is what we fight for. A little patriotism in Canada wouldn't hurt.

Ask any athlete who has competed for Canada in international competitions, and they will tell you of their pride in representing our country. They may be gay, of colour, of any religion, but what they are proud of, first and foremost, is Canada. Think of those 100,000 soldiers who fought at Vimy: they were Canadians from every region of our country including First Nations. They were Canadians of all religions, all linguistic groups, every sexual orientation. But the moment when the whistle blew and they had to go over the top of their trench, all they were and all they needed to be was Canadian.

***

While we're bolstering our patriotism, we might also give some thought to rehabilitating the notion of public service in Canada. I'll make this argument by quoting an American. "Ask not what your country can do for you, ask what you can do for your country," said John F. Kennedy in his oft-quoted 1961 inaugural address. It was all about service, a value that needs to be an honourable ambition in our country, too. As discussed earlier, Canada has produced outstanding citizens and still does. But service to country isn't encouraged in classrooms or valued highly enough throughout society. It has fallen out of favour in our "me-first" culture. Service to others, to your country, to humanity is a noble aspiration. The obligation to give back for a life filled with blessings, peace, and good fortune should not be a novel concept.

During my service in France in the late 1970s, the relationship between the country and its armed forces was called *Armées-Nation*. It stemmed from the country's mandatory military service, and it tied the populace to the military. Young men (only men at that time) were conscripted for twelve months of service in whatever unit they chose. Every man I encountered, even those of my vintage, had at one point served in the military. They had given that year for their country and understood the duty of service that came with living in a blessed, fortunate country like France.

My wife and I both served in our armed forces and two of my children continue that tradition. This represents some eighty-five collective years of service and counting. I am very proud of my family's commitment and respect and appreciate all who serve to protect our country. I truly think the moral contract described above must be appreciated by Canadians, and I also am aware that should Canada be attacked today or our values be threatened, I would expect my children to be prepared to put their lives on the line. I would hope all Canadians feel the same.

Aside from military service, our first responders provide an important service to Canadians and we could not do without them. Our medical professionals, firefighters, coast guards, and educators should also be saluted for their service. Even ordinary Canadians who tirelessly volunteer at hospitals, animal shelters, libraries, food banks, and neighbourhood groups must be recognized. Politicians at all levels serve their constituents and often do so with very little thanks or appreciation. Though some do not think of it as service, they *are* serving and we need to respect them and be grateful for their sacrifice. For my part, I always try to remember to thank them, even those who represent parties and ideals I do not support or whose opinions I do not share.

Conclusion

CANADIANS NEED TO BE shaken out of their complacency. Others have spoken and written about this dangerous way of thinking, in Canada and elsewhere. We need more outrage. Canadians seem happy to go on without a care, happy to let the government make decisions for them without so much as offering an opinion. We seem to exist, seemingly safe and oblivious, in our own personal bubbles within a larger national bubble.

Perhaps this situation has been exacerbated by the pandemic, fuelled by social distancing. I always thought "social distancing" was the wrong term. We should have called it *physical* distancing and reinforced *social* interaction. The pandemic may have waned, but individuals remain more introverted and therefore more complacent. Introverts became hermits and extroverts became introverts.

We need Canadians to emerge from this bubble with open eyes and ears, to experience this amazing country and the wider world, and to participate in society. We need Canadians to have opinions, we need them to discuss these opinions without fear of ridicule or cancellation, and we need to expose them to other opinions so they can flex their muscles of tolerance and understanding. And, as I have said often, we need Canadians to vote.

My good friend Dominique Trinquand, of whom I spoke earlier, is now a retired brigadier-general, and he decried the complacency of today's contented young French citizen, always happy to benefit from government handouts but unmotivated by hard work. "Let us firmly take measures that will allow us to live in a world where our comfort will not threaten nature," he said, "where democracy will not lead to weakness and where peace will reign because we will have defended it." I say amen.

Canada can return to being the best country in the world, but our citizens have to believe in it and have to have pride in it and have to want to be Canadian first, before being French, English, Irish, Iranian, Chinese, Indian, or First Nation. They must have pride in having absorbed the values of our country. Citizens must put Canada first and be overwhelmingly proud of belonging to this superb country; thereafter, they can be proud of and share their roots.

Our country has shown in the past that it can both look after its citizens and contribute internationally. Today, our leaders need to unite us and inspire a grand vision that will make Canada the envy of the world. We should be prepared to serve our country and be proud to do so.

Barbara and I did deliver that speech on the opening night of the CPC convention in September 2023. In the days and weeks that followed I realized that we had struck a chord with thousands of Canadians who felt about Canada the way we did. Like me, they are patriots and are ready to stand up for our country. I believe Canada stands at an inflection point. With all its resources, human and natural, its passion for the rule of law, and its values of peace, order, and good government, our country has the potential to return to greatness. Canadians will either achieve their potential or continue on the road to mediocrity. The above prescriptions for our country may not solve all our ills, but I believe they can help make Canada the best nation in the world. With leadership and service, Canada can achieve these lofty goals. And our leaders must share this vision and lead us to greatness.

"If not us, who? If not now, when?"

About the Author

MICHEL MAISONNEUVE COMPLETED 35 years of active service in the Canadian Armed Forces in May 2007. A tank officer from 12e Régiment blindé du Canada, he served in many locales throughout Canada and for a total of 10 years outside the country on operational missions and international positions, eventually rising to the rank of Lieutenant-General. Along the way, his exemplary service was recognized by awards from Canada, the U.S., France and NATO. Michel testified in The Hague against Slobodan Milosevic, commanded the funeral for the Unknown Soldier in Ottawa, was the last Chief of Staff of NATO's Supreme Allied Command Atlantic and the first Chief of Staff of NATO's Supreme Allied Command Transformation. After his service in uniform, he continued to serve Canada as the first Academic Director (Principal) of Royal Military College Saint-Jean on its re-opening in December 2007, and for more than 10 years afterwards, where he helped return the College to university status. He was named the 30th laureate of the Vimy Award in 2022 for his exceptional contribution to Canada's security and defence, and the preservation of its democratic values. On that occasion he gave a rousing speech that gained him the moniker "The Anti-Woke General" and upset some left-wing media and academics. A native and bilingual Quebecer, Michel is passionate about Veterans and serving military personnel, the

ABOUT THE AUTHOR

preservation of Canada's proud history, the importance of volunteerism, leadership and service in our country, and the freedom and willingness to participate in its development. A father of four, Michel and his wife Barbara live in Niagara with their very well-behaved little white dog Kevin. He tries to keep in shape by walking and stays humble by playing golf badly. He enjoys the occasional cigar, a dram of scotch, and solving the world's problems in great conversation with friends.